All Kinds of AIRPLANES

by Maurice Allward
illustrated by John Young

GROSSET & DUNLAP · Publishers · NEW YORK
A NATIONAL GENERAL COMPANY

First Planes to Fly

Man has made many attempts to fly, and until 1903 the most successful of his inventions was the balloon. However, the balloon, at the mercy of air currents, proved difficult to control.

Experiments were made to build a "heavier-than-air" machine that would fly, and in 1903, the Wright brothers were successful.

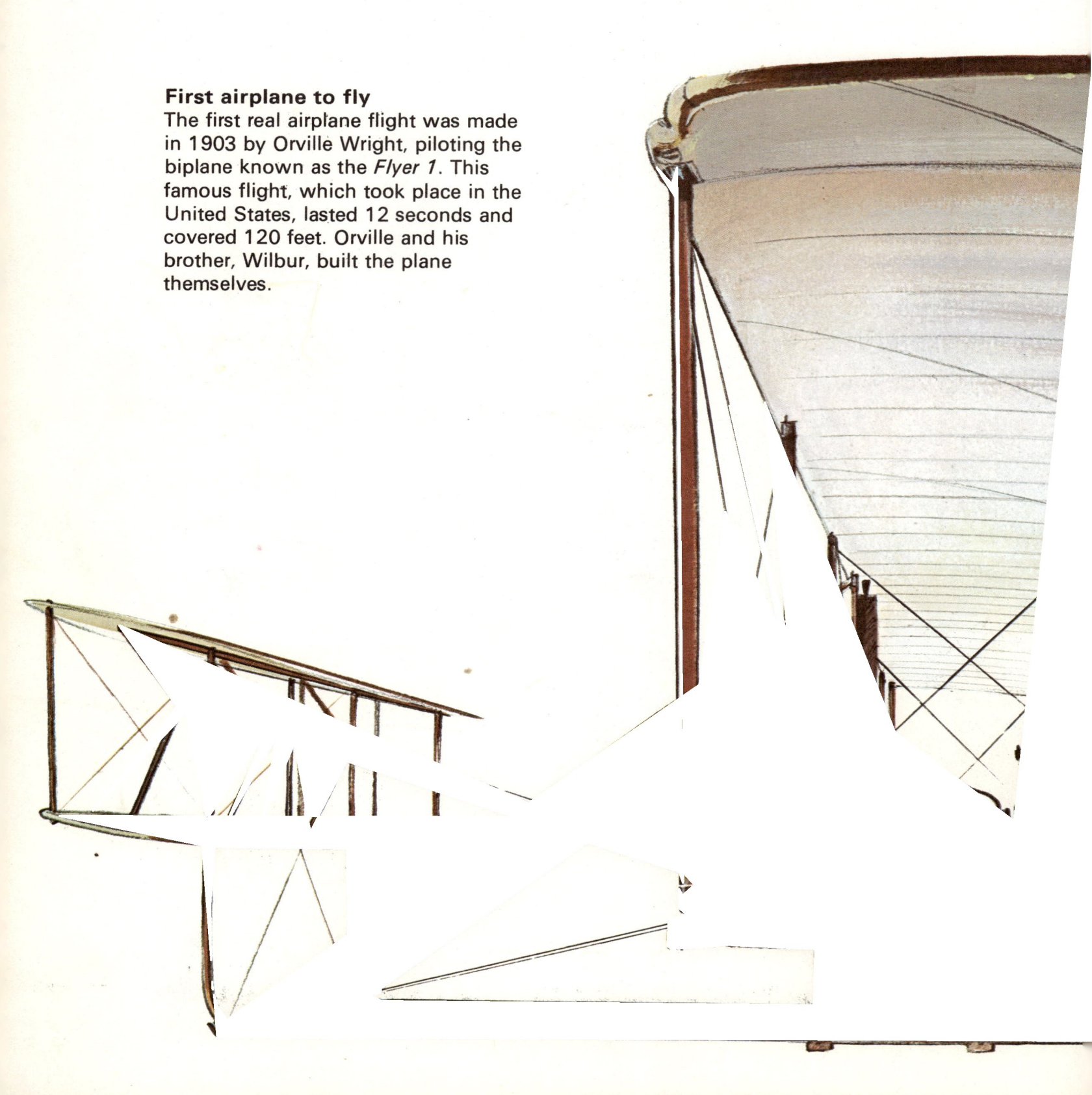

First airplane to fly
The first real airplane flight was made in 1903 by Orville Wright, piloting the biplane known as the *Flyer 1*. This famous flight, which took place in the United States, lasted 12 seconds and covered 120 feet. Orville and his brother, Wilbur, built the plane themselves.

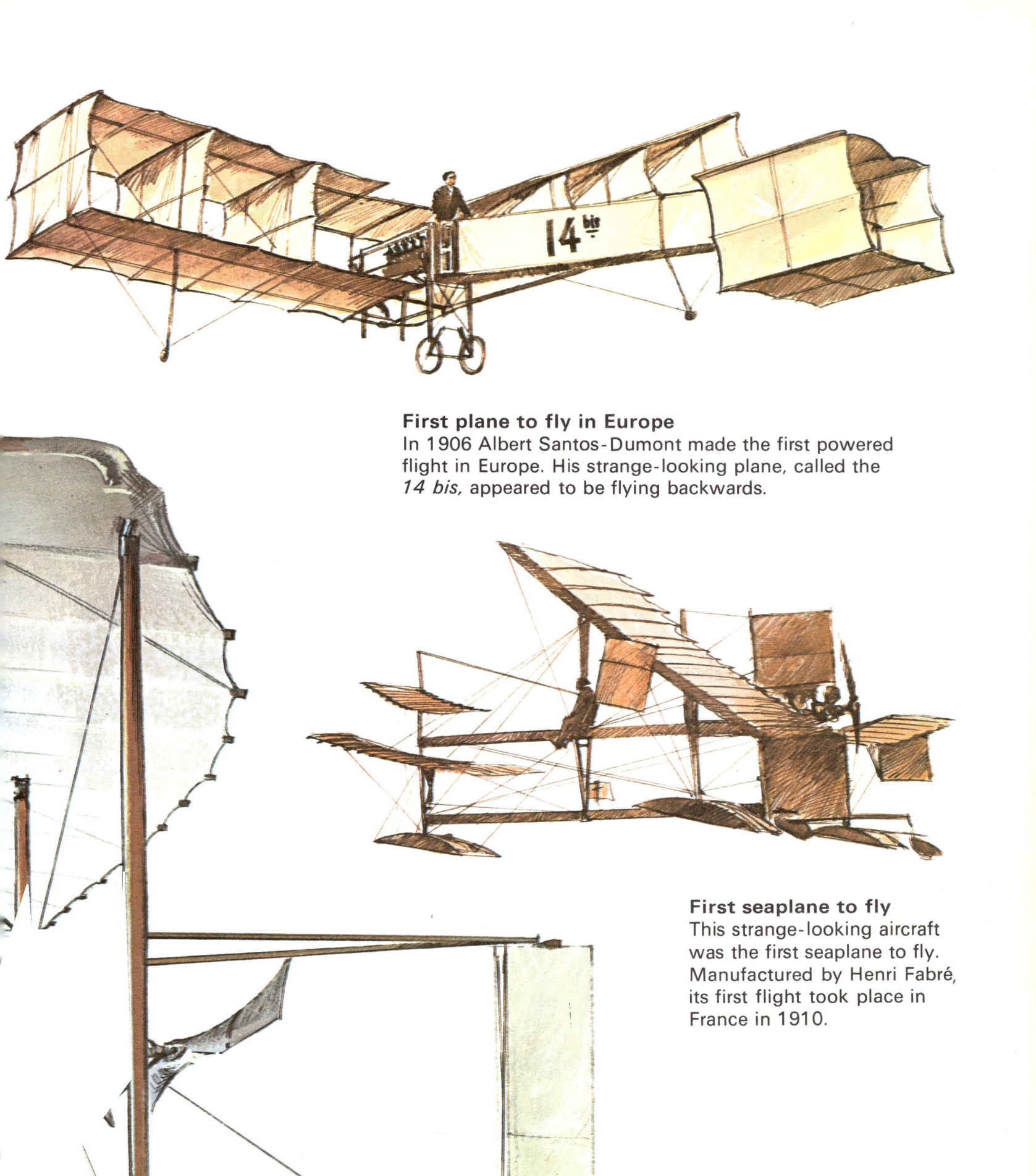

First plane to fly in Europe
In 1906 Albert Santos-Dumont made the first powered flight in Europe. His strange-looking plane, called the *14 bis,* appeared to be flying backwards.

First seaplane to fly
This strange-looking aircraft was the first seaplane to fly. Manufactured by Henri Fabré, its first flight took place in France in 1910.

Three-winged Airplanes

Most early airplanes had either one or two wings. A few had three and were fairly successful. Here are some of them.

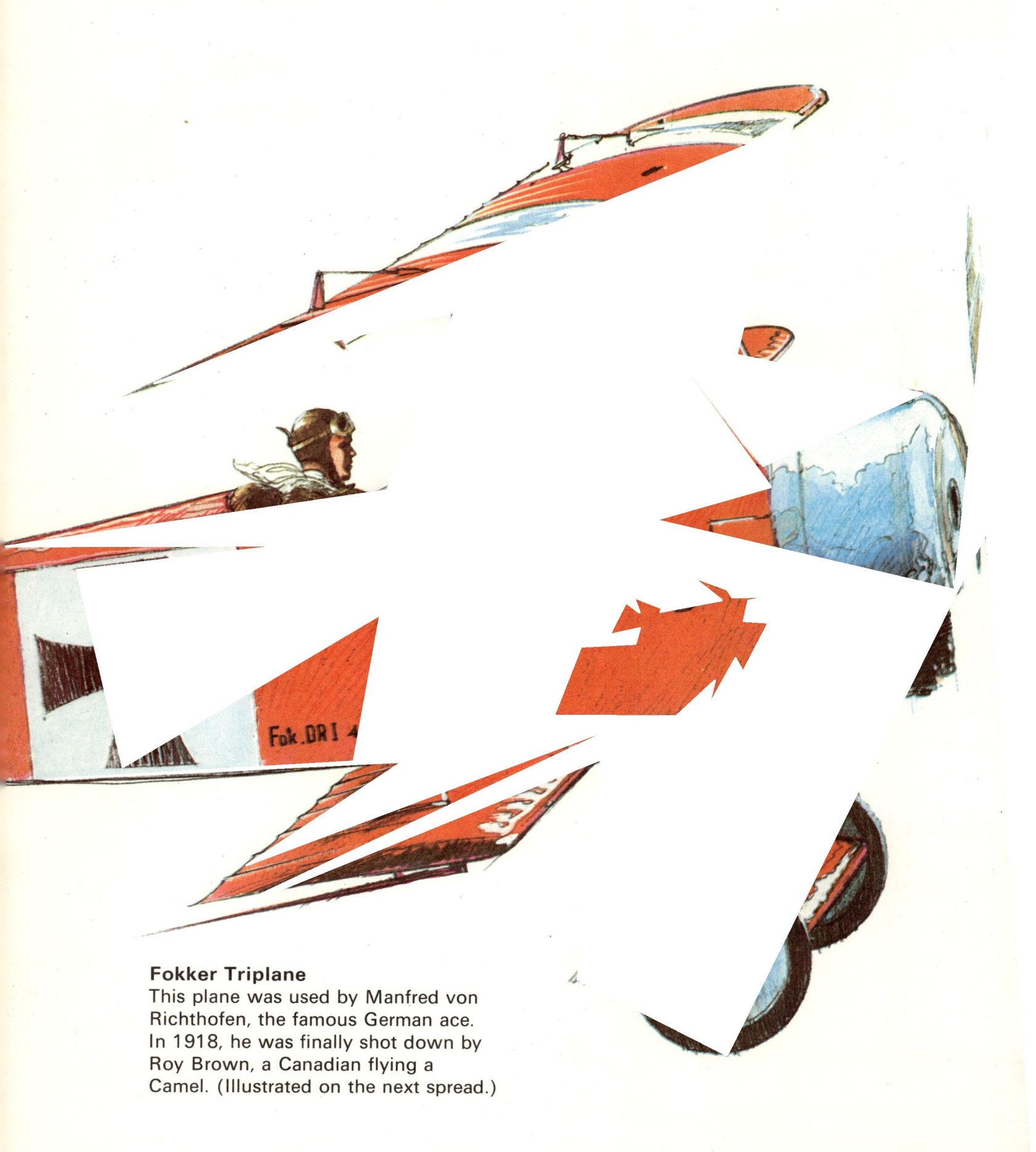

Fokker Triplane
This plane was used by Manfred von Richthofen, the famous German ace. In 1918, he was finally shot down by Roy Brown, a Canadian flying a Camel. (Illustrated on the next spread.)

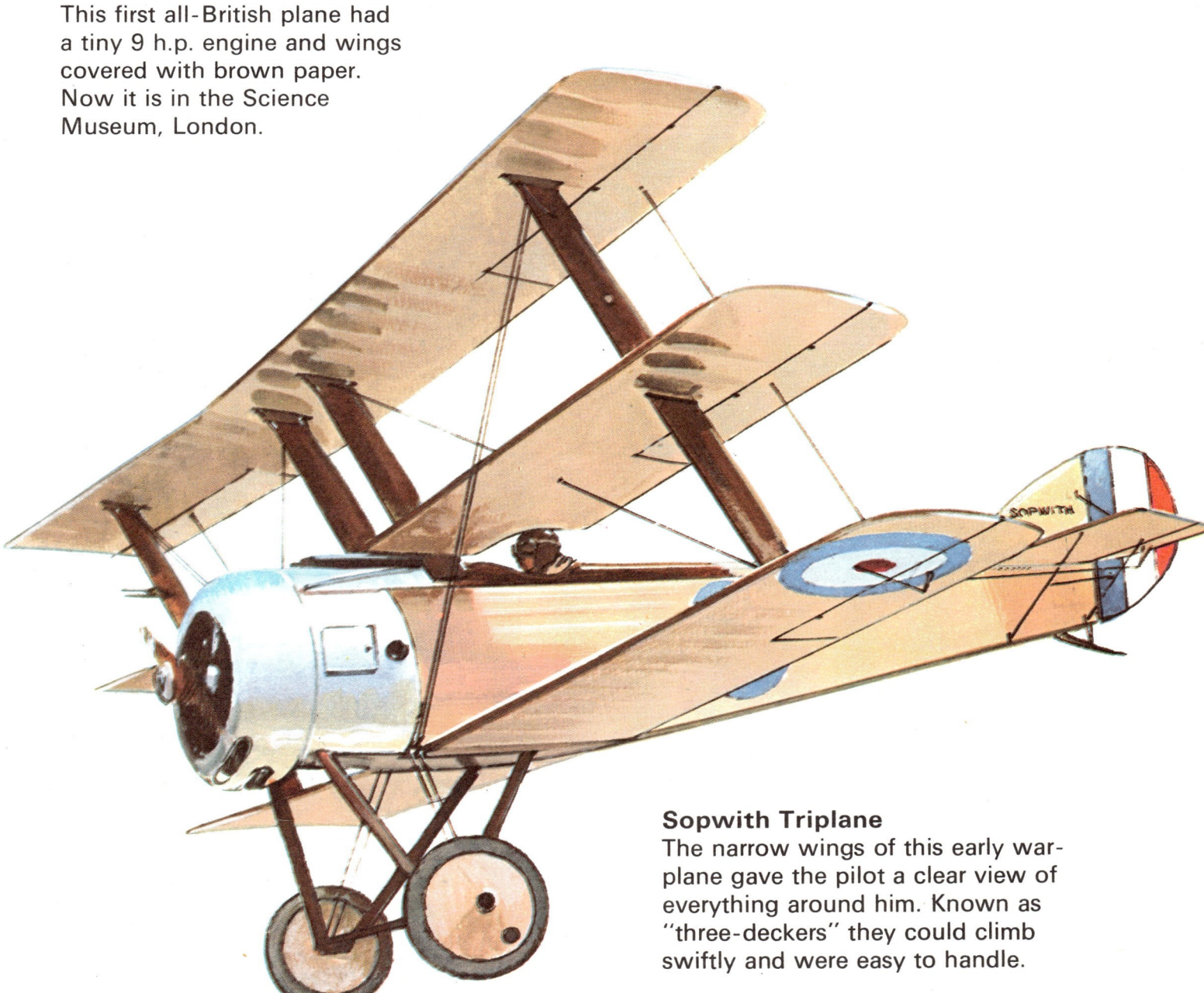

Avro Triplane
This first all-British plane had a tiny 9 h.p. engine and wings covered with brown paper. Now it is in the Science Museum, London.

Sopwith Triplane
The narrow wings of this early warplane gave the pilot a clear view of everything around him. Known as "three-deckers" they could climb swiftly and were easy to handle.

Early War Planes

Planes were soon used in war. At first, unarmed planes were sent to scout behind enemy lines, but soon guns were fitted and the first bombing raids began. Later, specially designed fighter and bomber planes were built.

Morane-Saulnier Parasol
Over 600 of these French fighters served with the French, British and Russian air forces. One of their most impressive feats was the destruction of the Zeppelin LZ 37 in June, 1915.

Sopwith Camel
This British fighter was used in the First World War. It was easy to handle and could change direction very quickly. Armed with two machine guns, this type of aircraft shot down 1,294 enemy aircraft: more than any other fighter.

Gotha
This big German bomber was used in raids against England during the First World War, and even bombed London in daylight. As illustrated, the rear-gunner fired through an opening in the bottom of the fuselage.

Early Passenger Aircraft

After the First World War, people began to use aircraft for peaceful purposes. At first they were used for carrying mail, and then passengers.

Dakota
This is the most famous passenger aircraft of all. The first one flew in 1935. Over 10,000 were built, and many of the later models are still being used today.

De Havilland DH 34
The De Havilland DH 34 carried eleven people — nine passengers, and two pilots in an open cockpit. Powered by a 450 h.p. Napier Lion engine, this pioneer airliner had a cruising speed of 105 m.p.h. and a range of 365 miles.

Junkers 52
This three-engined, seventeen passenger airliner was used as Germany's standard troop-transport aircraft during the 1939-45 war.

Famous Planes

There are some aircraft that have become as famous as their pilots — Alcock and Brown and the Vickers Vimy or Lindbergh and the "Spirit of St. Louis". Three of them are illustrated below.

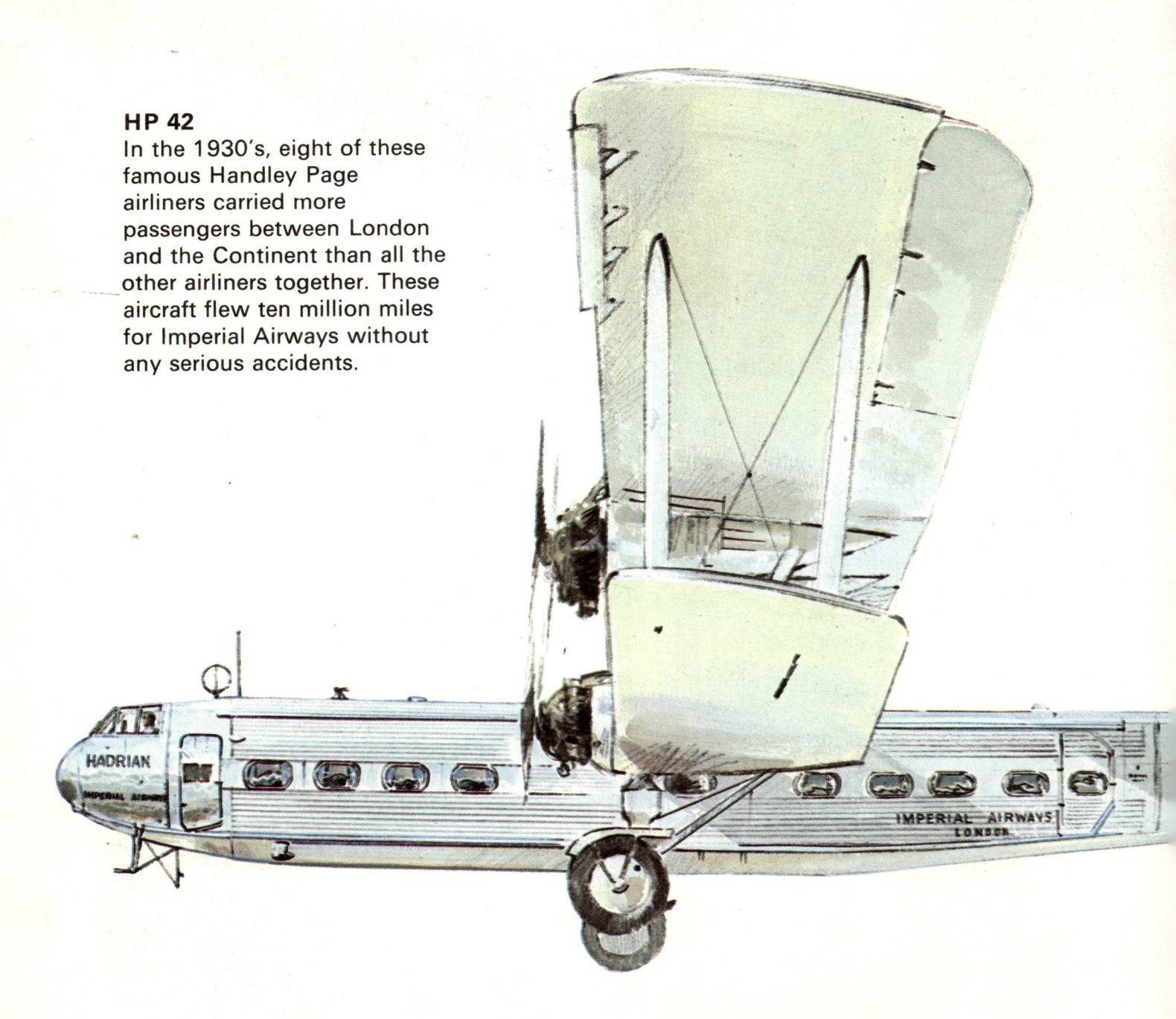

HP 42
In the 1930's, eight of these famous Handley Page airliners carried more passengers between London and the Continent than all the other airliners together. These aircraft flew ten million miles for Imperial Airways without any serious accidents.

"Spirit of St. Louis"
This small Ryan airplane was used by a young pilot named Charles Lindbergh, to fly non-stop from the United States to Paris, in 1927. The 3,600-mile trip took 33 hours and made Lindbergh and his aircraft world-famous.

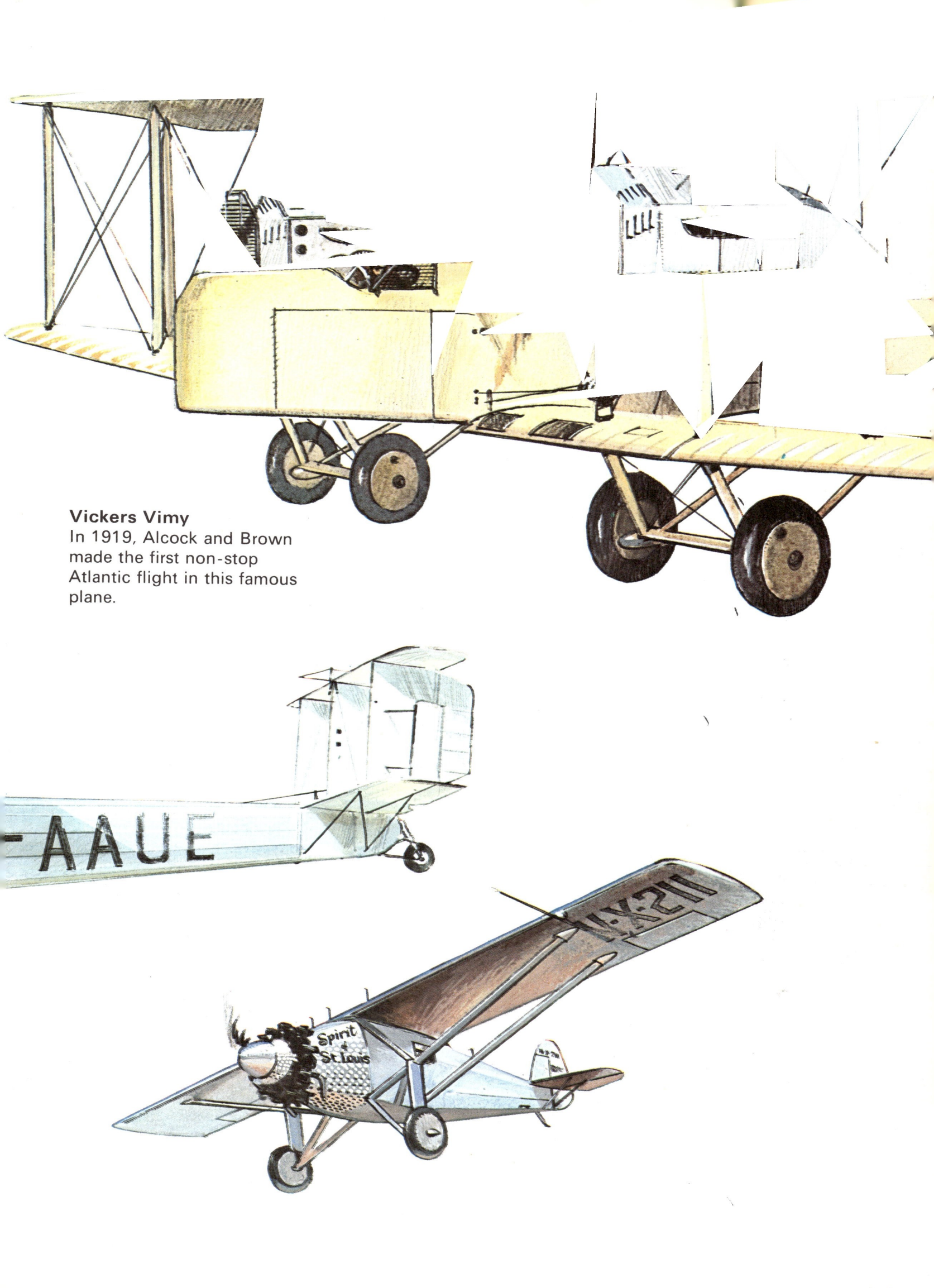

Vickers Vimy
In 1919, Alcock and Brown made the first non-stop Atlantic flight in this famous plane.

The Battle of Britain

In the summer of 1940, a great battle was fought in the skies between the Royal Air Force and the *Luftwaffe.* Germany lost the battle and this had an important effect on the result of the war.

Messerschmitt Me 109
The Me 109, armed with one cannon and two machine-guns, was the main German fighter of the Battle of Britain.

Heinkel He 111
This German bomber had a range of 1,740 miles and could carry as much as two tons of bombs.

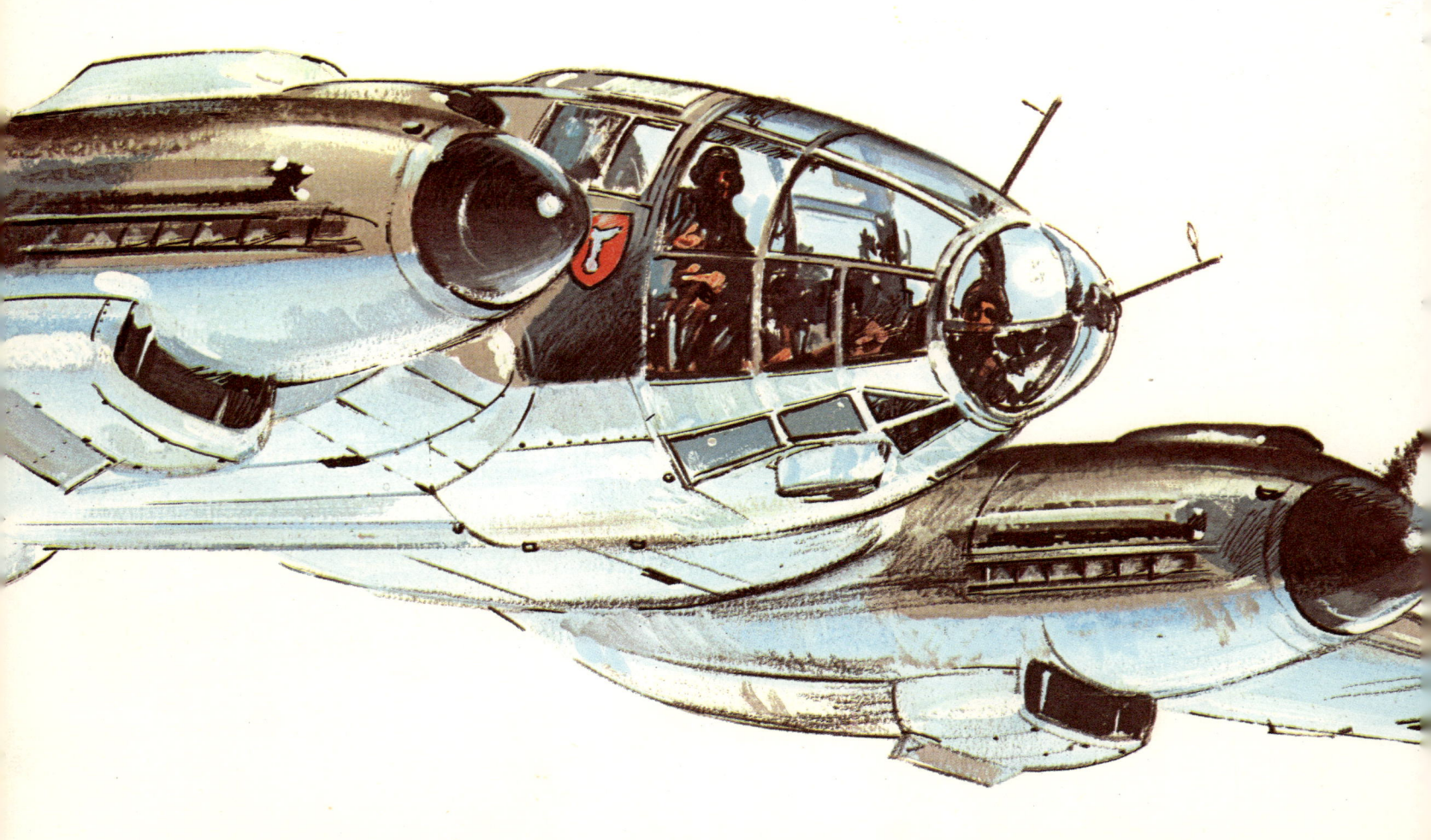

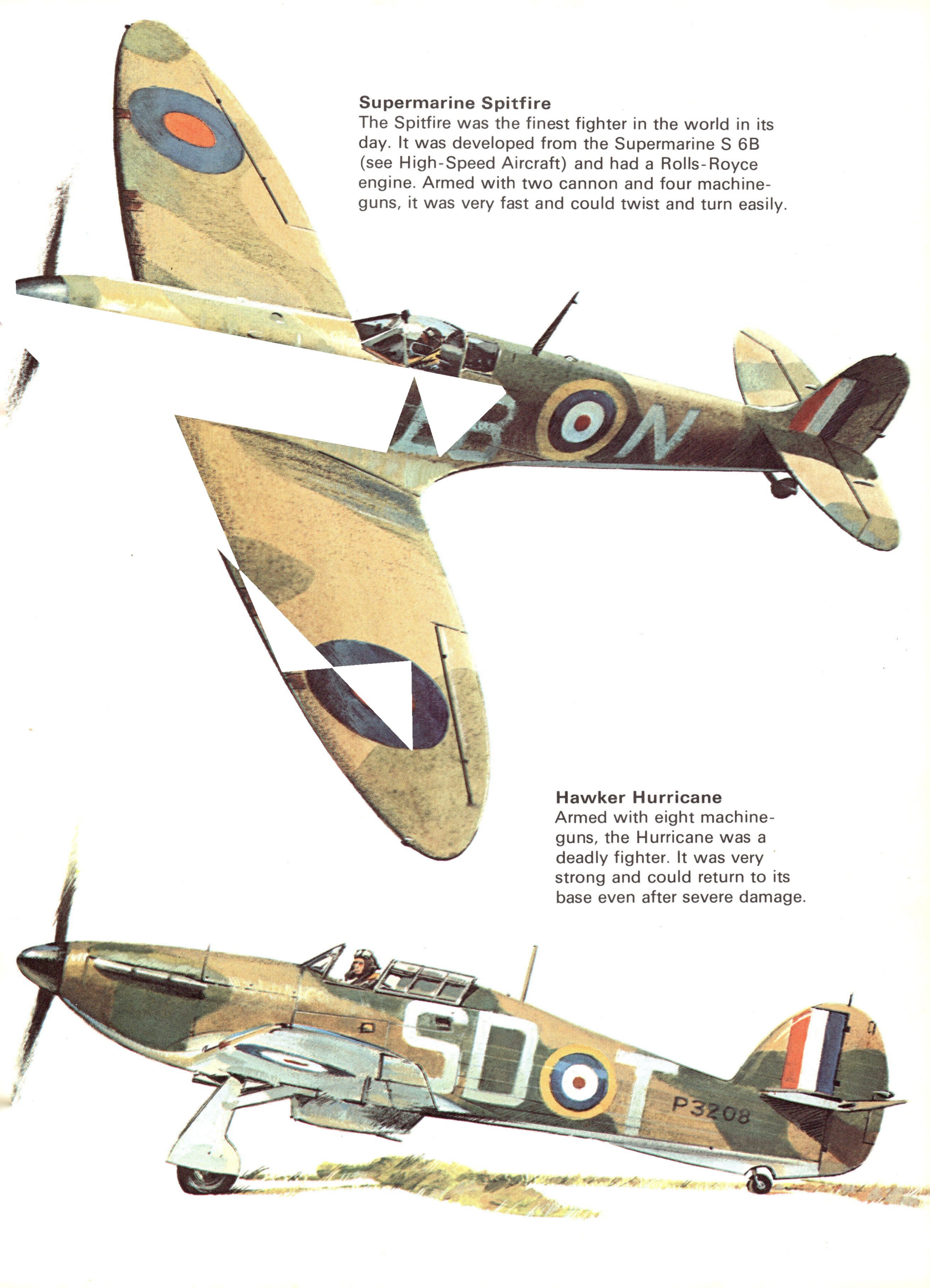

Supermarine Spitfire
The Spitfire was the finest fighter in the world in its day. It was developed from the Supermarine S 6B (see High-Speed Aircraft) and had a Rolls-Royce engine. Armed with two cannon and four machine-guns, it was very fast and could twist and turn easily.

Hawker Hurricane
Armed with eight machine-guns, the Hurricane was a deadly fighter. It was very strong and could return to its base even after severe damage.

Flying Boats

Modern airports around the world have made development of flying-boats unnecessary. A few are still used for military purposes and other special tasks.

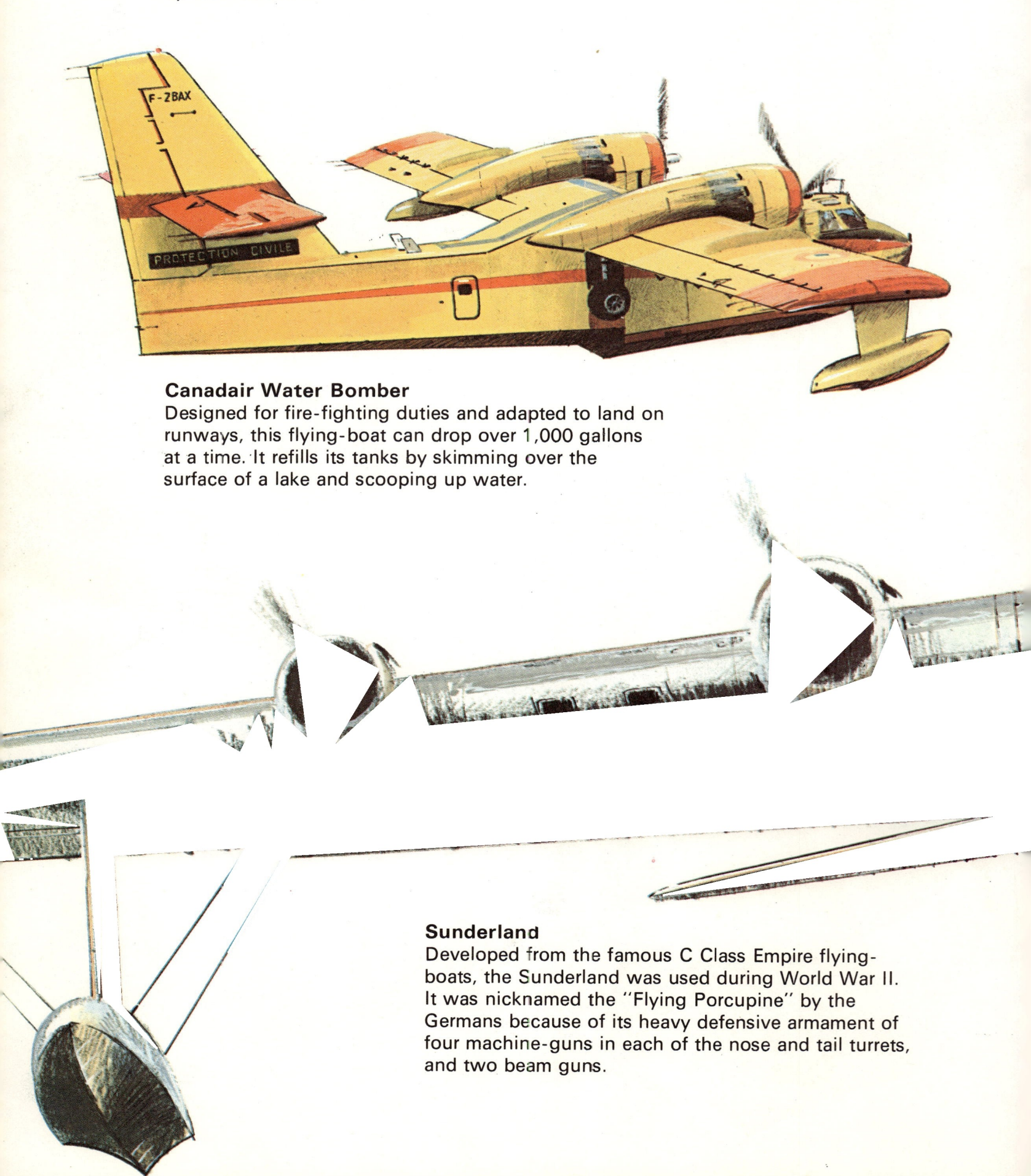

Canadair Water Bomber
Designed for fire-fighting duties and adapted to land on runways, this flying-boat can drop over 1,000 gallons at a time. It refills its tanks by skimming over the surface of a lake and scooping up water.

Sunderland
Developed from the famous C Class Empire flying-boats, the Sunderland was used during World War II. It was nicknamed the "Flying Porcupine" by the Germans because of its heavy defensive armament of four machine-guns in each of the nose and tail turrets, and two beam guns.

Princess
The Princess was the finest flying-boat ever built, but was never brought into service. It was dismantled in 1967.

Fighter Aircraft

Some of the fastest planes are the fighters. These are planes carrying guns. They are used to intercept and shoot down enemy aircraft. Most fighters can also carry bombs, if necessary.

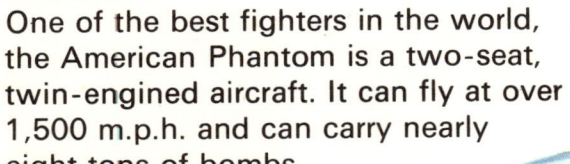

Phantom
One of the best fighters in the world, the American Phantom is a two-seat, twin-engined aircraft. It can fly at over 1,500 m.p.h. and can carry nearly eight tons of bombs.

Mirage
This successful French fighter can fly at 1,430 m.p.h. and is armed with two cannon and rockets. It can carry up to fourteen bombs under the fuselage and wings, for attacking targets on the ground.

Lightning
Powered by two Rolls-Royce engines, this British fighter can fly at 1,500 m.p.h. It is armed with two cannon and rockets.

Bombers

In the early days, pilots dropped their bombs over the side of the plane. Now, specially designed aircraft carry their deadly load of bombs inside the fuselage or under the wings.

Buccaneer
The Buccaneer is a British twin-jet bomber specially designed to fly fast and low, so that it can slip under the radar screens of an enemy.

Stratofortress
This giant American bomber — the B.52, can carry many tons of bombs and fly for 12,500 miles without refuelling. It can also carry guided missiles under its wings.

Bear
This huge Russian bomber is driven by four powerful turbo-prop engines. It can carry about eleven tons of bombs, and has a range of 8,000 miles.

Aircraft for hunting Submarines

Submarines are dangerous and difficult to find as they move beneath the surface of the vast oceans which cover nearly three-quarters of the Earth's surface. Special aircraft have been built to detect and attack submarines.

Nimrod
The only jet-powered submarine hunter, based on the famous Comet airliner, the Nimrod can carry a wide range of anti-submarine weapons. Its four powerful Rolls-Royce jet engines give it a long range and high speed.

Orion
Developed from the Electra airliner, the Orion can carry a heavy load of depth charges, mines, torpedoes and missiles. The sting in the tail contains magnetic equipment to detect submarines while they are submerged.

Atlantic
Specially designed to hunt submarines, the Atlantic carries depth charges, homing torpedoes and missiles with atomic warheads in its large bomb bay.

Planes that help Farmers

One of the many useful tasks that airplanes carry out for farmers is the spraying of crops. Airplanes are used for spreading fertilizers and chemical compounds that prevent the spread of disease. Because the pilot has to fly low, crop spraying is dangerous and requires great skill.

Cessna 180
In addition to spraying crops, aircraft help farmers by dropping food to livestock cut off by snow or floods.

AgCat
This highly successful American biplane has been specially built for crop spraying. The large fairing protects the pilot in case the aircraft turns over.

Piper Pawnee
The Pawnee is specially designed for crop spraying, from either a central hopper or from spray bars fitted under the wings. The fuselage is specially designed to protect the pilot in the event of a crash.

Do-it-yourself Aircraft

A do-it-yourself enthusiast can build a small, simple plane in his own workshop or garage. Detailed drawings and, sometimes, a kit of parts are supplied by the manufacturer.

Druine Turbi
This popular French do-it-yourself aircraft has been built by amateurs all over the world. Many of them are powered by Volkswagen car engines.

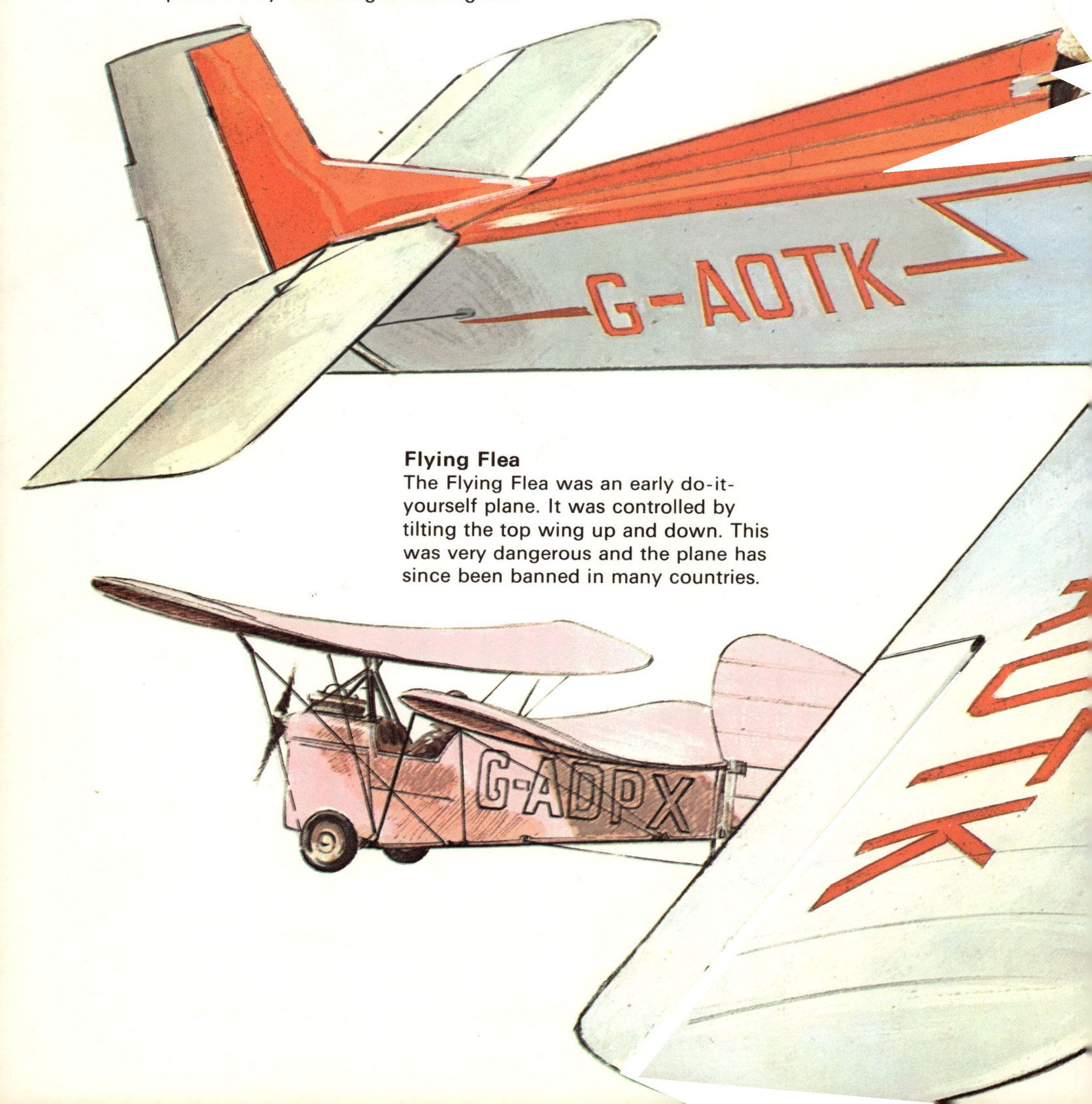

Flying Flea
The Flying Flea was an early do-it-yourself plane. It was controlled by tilting the top wing up and down. This was very dangerous and the plane has since been banned in many countries.

Starduster
Several of these single-seat, sporting biplanes, have been built by amateurs in America. They can fly at 150 m.p.h.

Trainers

Training aircraft must be fairly easy to fly and yet demand a degree of skill from their pupils, otherwise they do not make good trainers. The right combination of ease and skill is not easy to achieve.

Avro 504
The Avro 504 is remembered as one of the best trainers of all. It was an outstanding aircraft. Over 8,000 were built during 1914-18. The aircraft illustrated has 1919 Danish Army markings.

Gnat
The Gnat Trainer is easy and pleasant to fly, and yet offers pupils the high-speed performance of jet fighters. The fantastic aerobatic teams of Gnats, such as the Red Arrows of the R.A.F. illustrated here, are a familiar sight at air shows.

Ryan PT
In 1939 the U.S. Army Air Corps adopted this two-seat trainer. It had a top speed of 150 m.p.h.

Talon
The Talon is a supersonic, lightweight, twin-jet advanced trainer. It has a top speed of 817 m.p.h. and is also used for training U.S. astronauts.

Planes for Aerobatics

Few sights are more thrilling than that of an airplane doing aerobatics high in a blue summer sky. Aerobatics not only require skill on the part of the pilot, but the plane must be specially designed to withstand the heavy stresses imposed upon it.

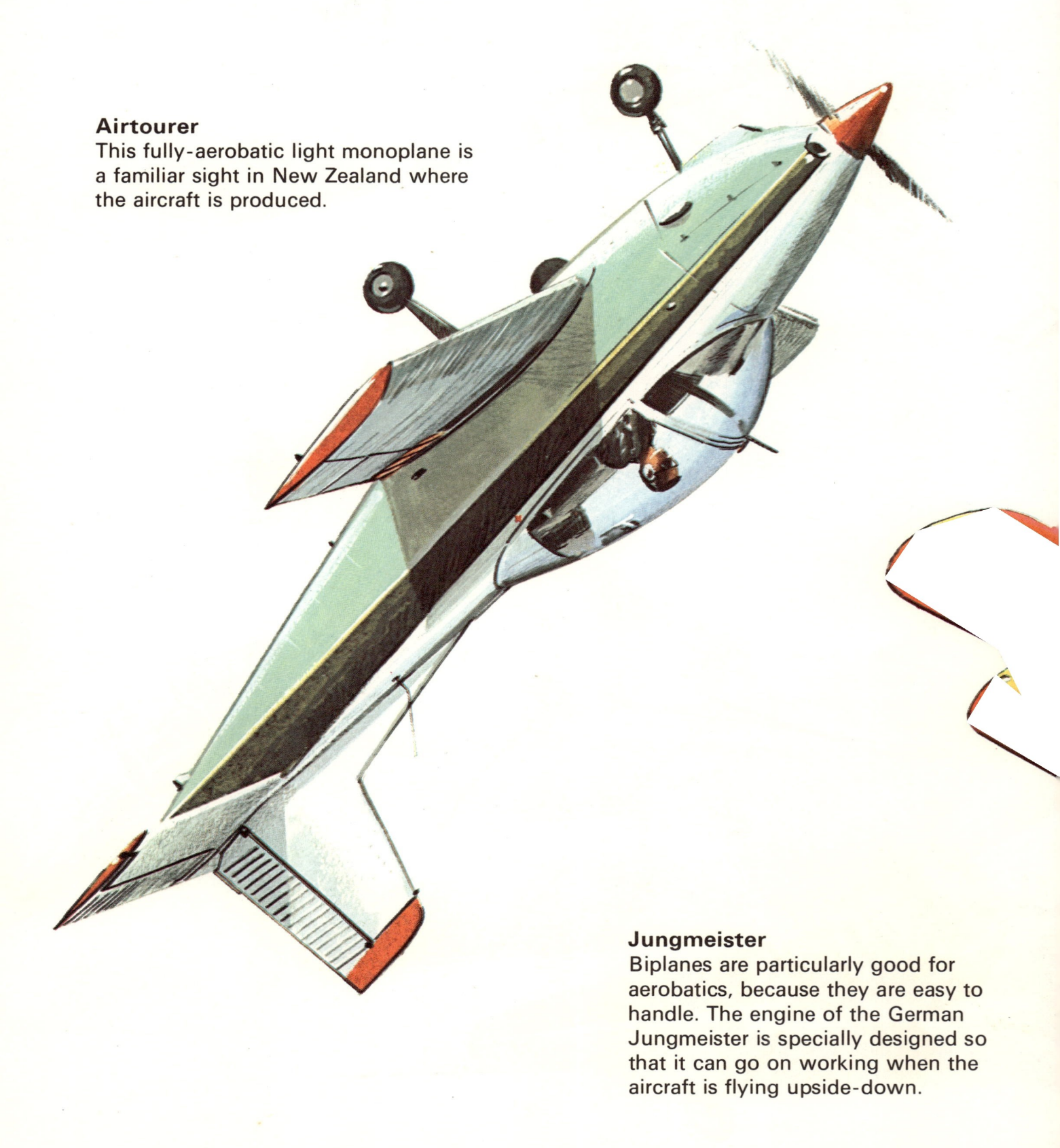

Airtourer
This fully-aerobatic light monoplane is a familiar sight in New Zealand where the aircraft is produced.

Jungmeister
Biplanes are particularly good for aerobatics, because they are easy to handle. The engine of the German Jungmeister is specially designed so that it can go on working when the aircraft is flying upside-down.

Zlin Trener
Built in Czechoslovakia, this popular plane can be used for training or aerobatics. Over 1,000 of these planes have been made and they have won many sporting championships.

Gliders

Gliding is a very popular sport. You can learn to fly a glider when you are sixteen years old! Lots of people start on a glider before training on powered aircraft. Skilled pilots can fly hundreds of miles in advanced types of gliders known as sailplanes.

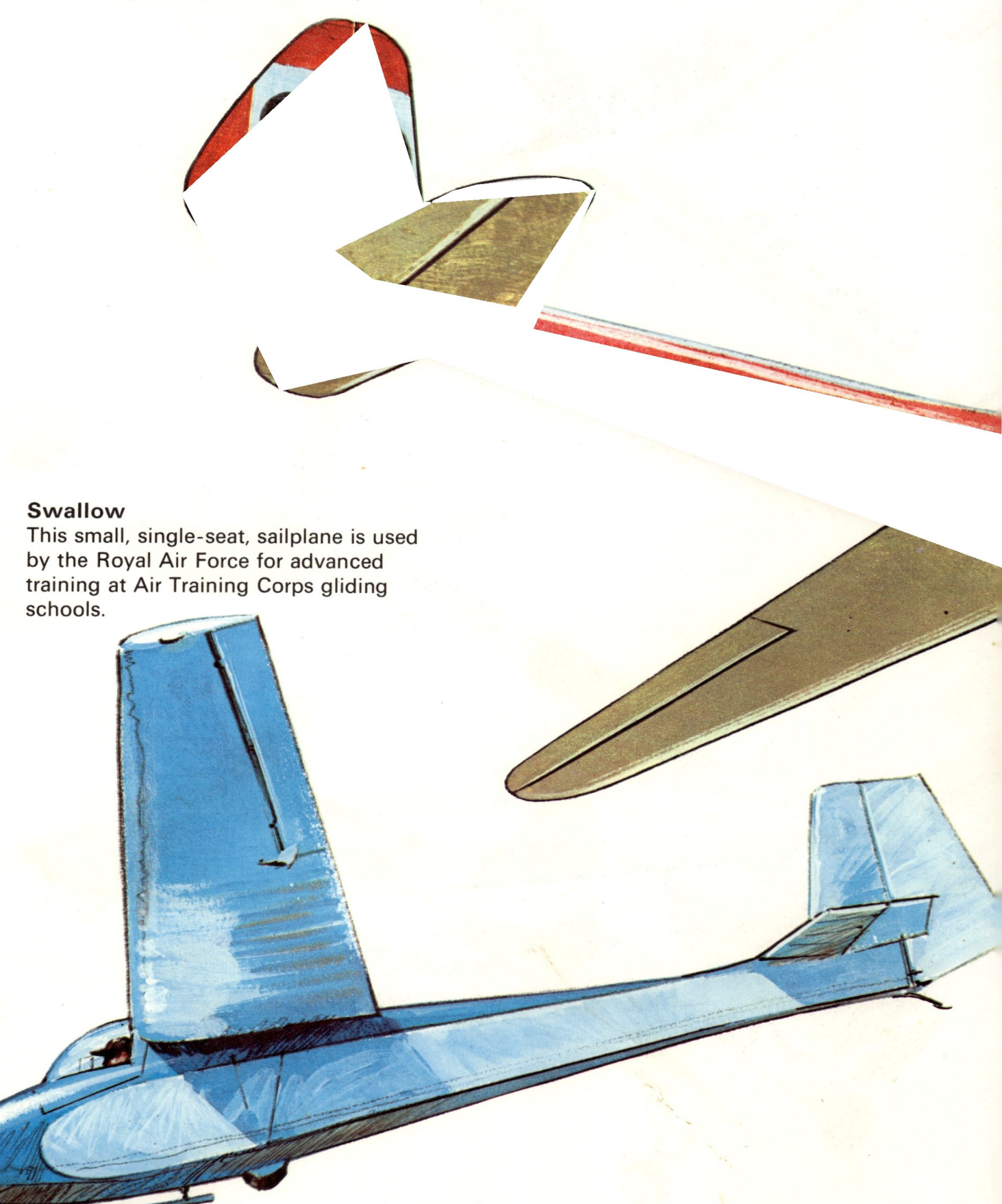

Swallow
This small, single-seat, sailplane is used by the Royal Air Force for advanced training at Air Training Corps gliding schools.

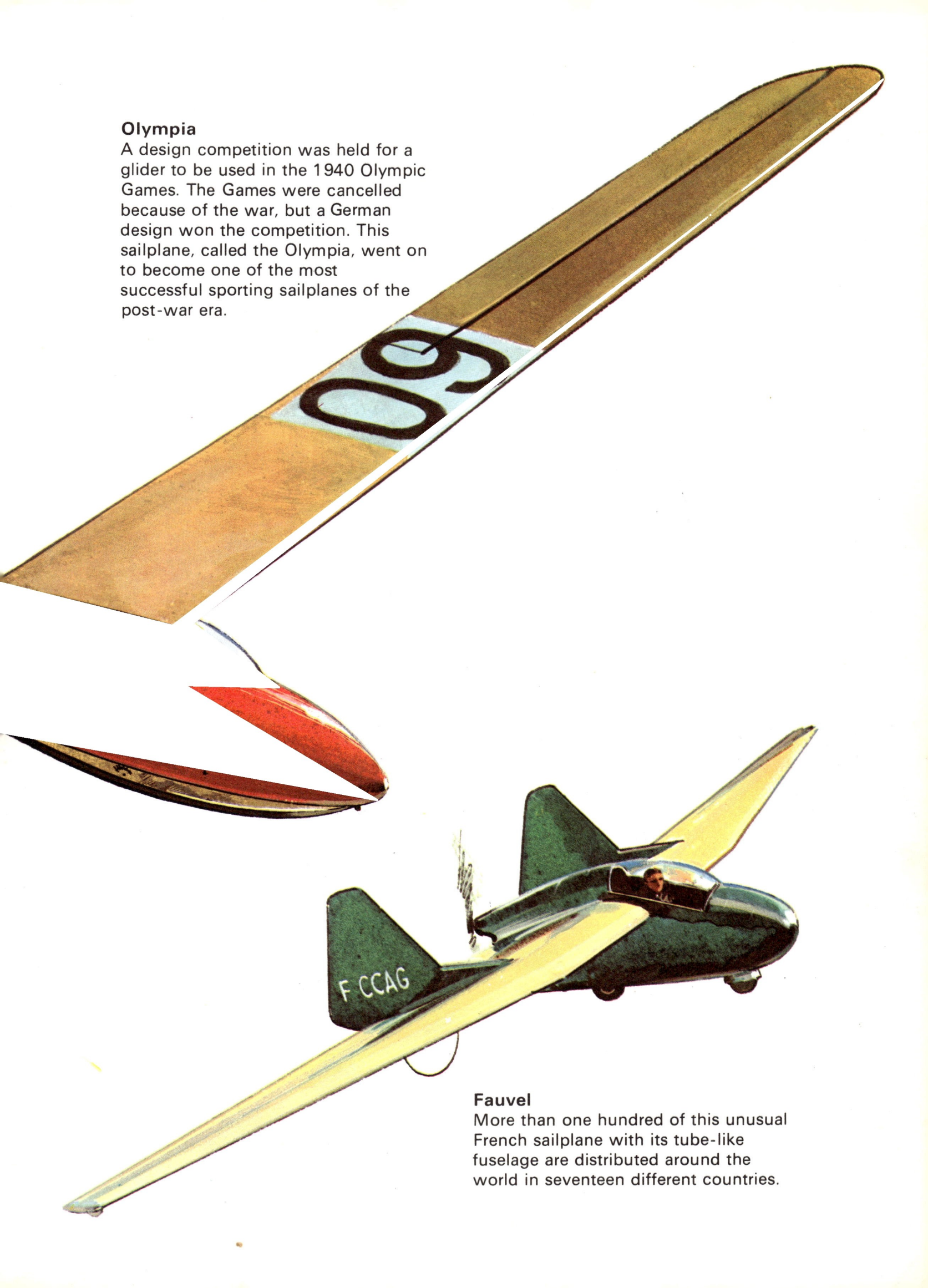

Olympia
A design competition was held for a glider to be used in the 1940 Olympic Games. The Games were cancelled because of the war, but a German design won the competition. This sailplane, called the Olympia, went on to become one of the most successful sporting sailplanes of the post-war era.

Fauvel
More than one hundred of this unusual French sailplane with its tube-like fuselage are distributed around the world in seventeen different countries.

Oddities of the Air

Aircraft designed for odd jobs sometimes have odd shapes. Often they do not look like airplanes at all and are built in a bewildering array of shapes and sizes.

Pogo
This extraordinary two-man rocket-propelled lifting platform has been specially designed for use on the moon.

Super Guppy
Designed to carry extra-large cargoes, such as parts of space rockets, the Super Guppy is based on the popular Boeing Stratocruiser airliner.

Jindivik
Because it is used as a radio-controlled flying target by other planes and rockets, there is no room for a pilot in this strange aircraft.

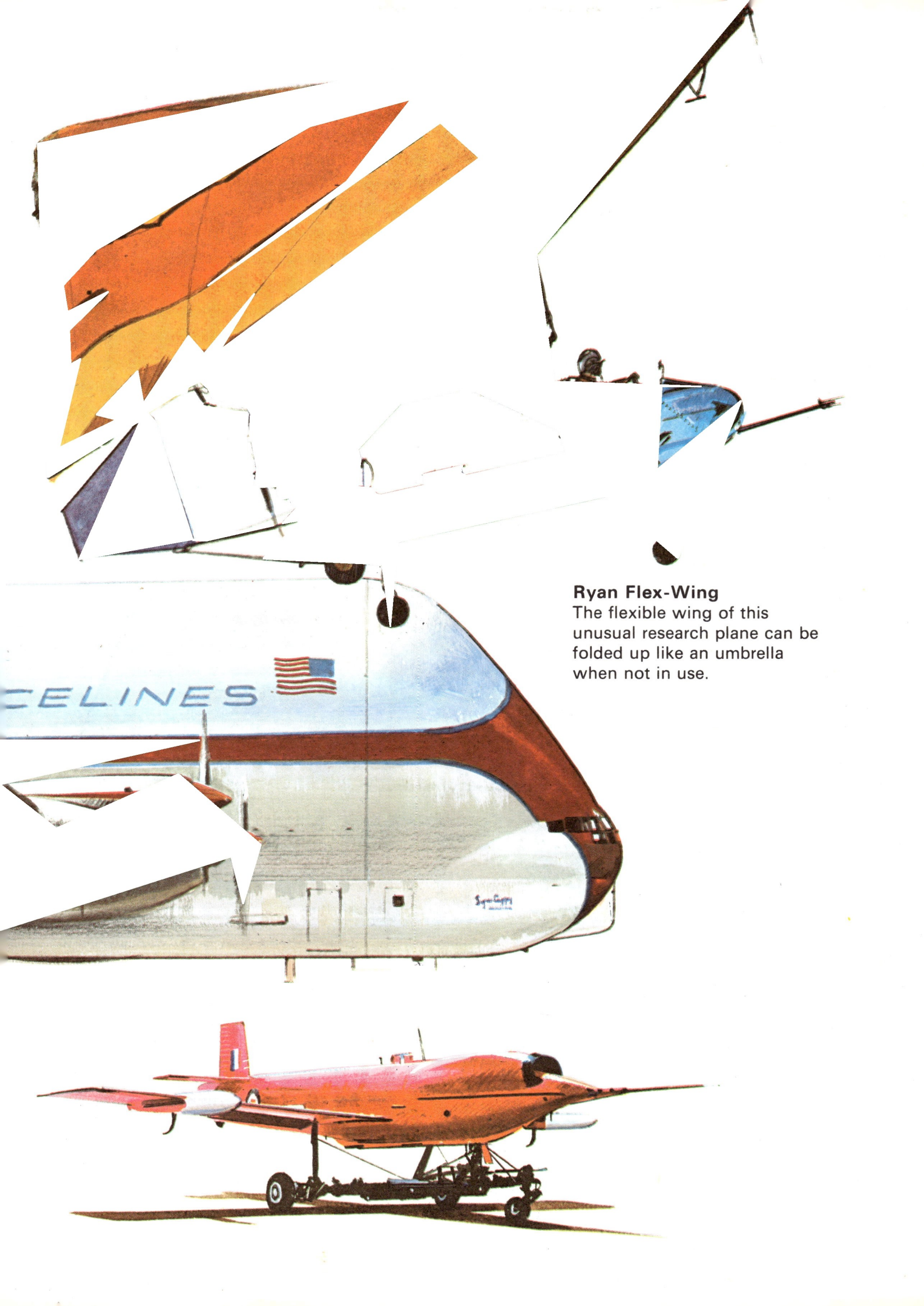

Ryan Flex-Wing
The flexible wing of this unusual research plane can be folded up like an umbrella when not in use.

Rotating-wing Aircraft

Although they are expensive to operate, compared with fixed-wing planes, rotating-wing aircraft are widely used where vertical take-off or hovering is required.

Cierva Autogiro
Juan de la Cierva built one of the first successful rotating-wing aircraft in 1923. His autogiro is not a true helicopter because its rotor is not powered.

Jet Ranger
Designed for civil duties, the Jet Ranger can carry five people. It can fly at 150 m.p.h. with an overall range of 390 miles.

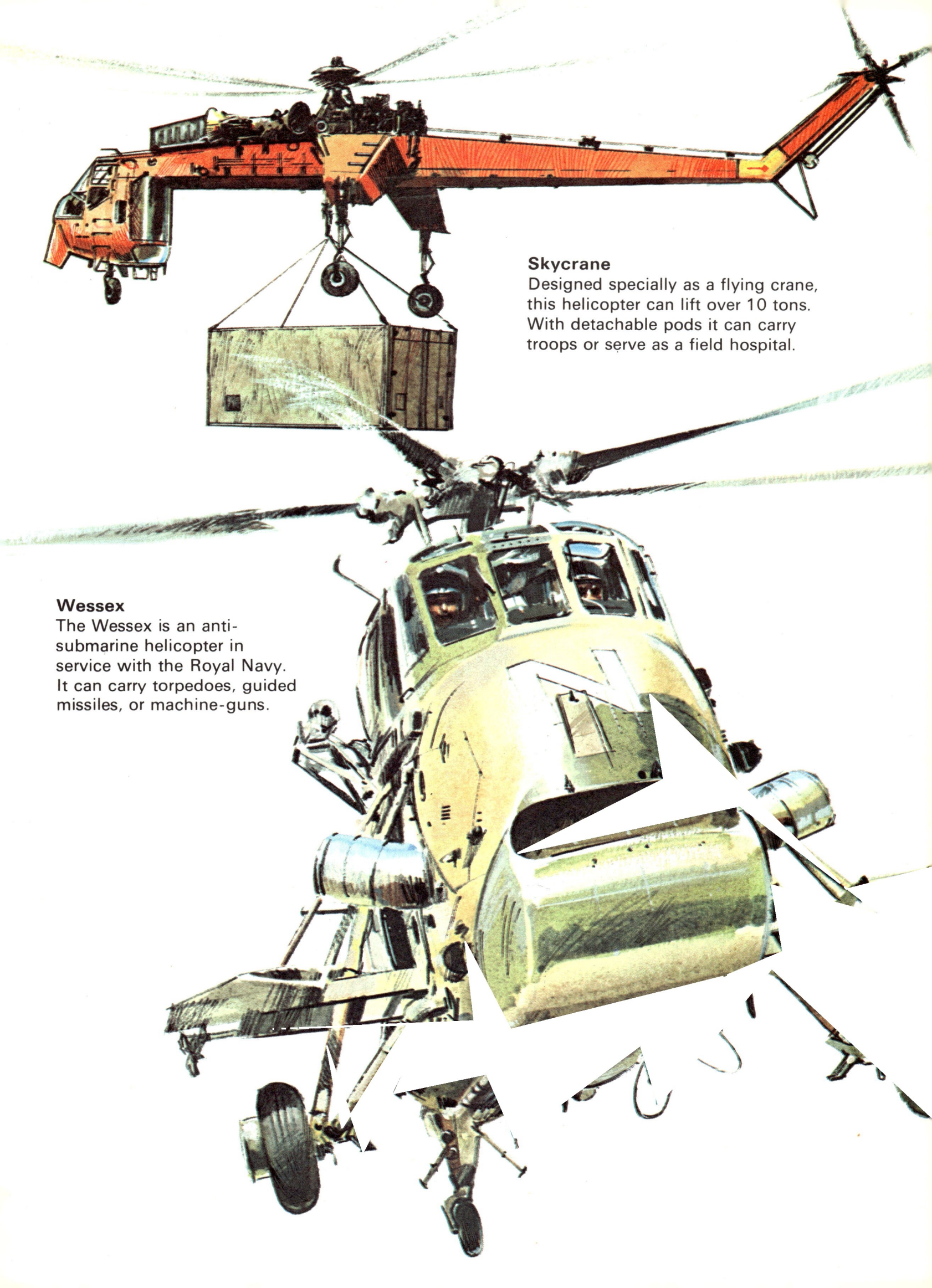

Skycrane
Designed specially as a flying crane, this helicopter can lift over 10 tons. With detachable pods it can carry troops or serve as a field hospital.

Wessex
The Wessex is an anti-submarine helicopter in service with the Royal Navy. It can carry torpedoes, guided missiles, or machine-guns.

Liners of the Air

Over three hundred million people now travel by air each year. Most of them fly in fast, smooth, jet airliners – three examples are shown here.

Boeing 727
The Boeing 727 is one of the most successful airliners of all time. It is powered by three jet engines.

VC 10
Favorite liner of the air with many passengers is the VC 10. Its four powerful Rolls-Royce Conway engines at the tail give a quiet, smooth ride.

Douglas DC-8
The latest versions of this successful airliner can carry up to 259 passengers. Illustrated here is an extended version in Air Jamaica colors.

High-speed Aircraft

Flying is much the fastest way to travel. High-speed planes are built for defense and reconnaissance duties, research, or quite simply to get passengers to their destination as quickly as possible.

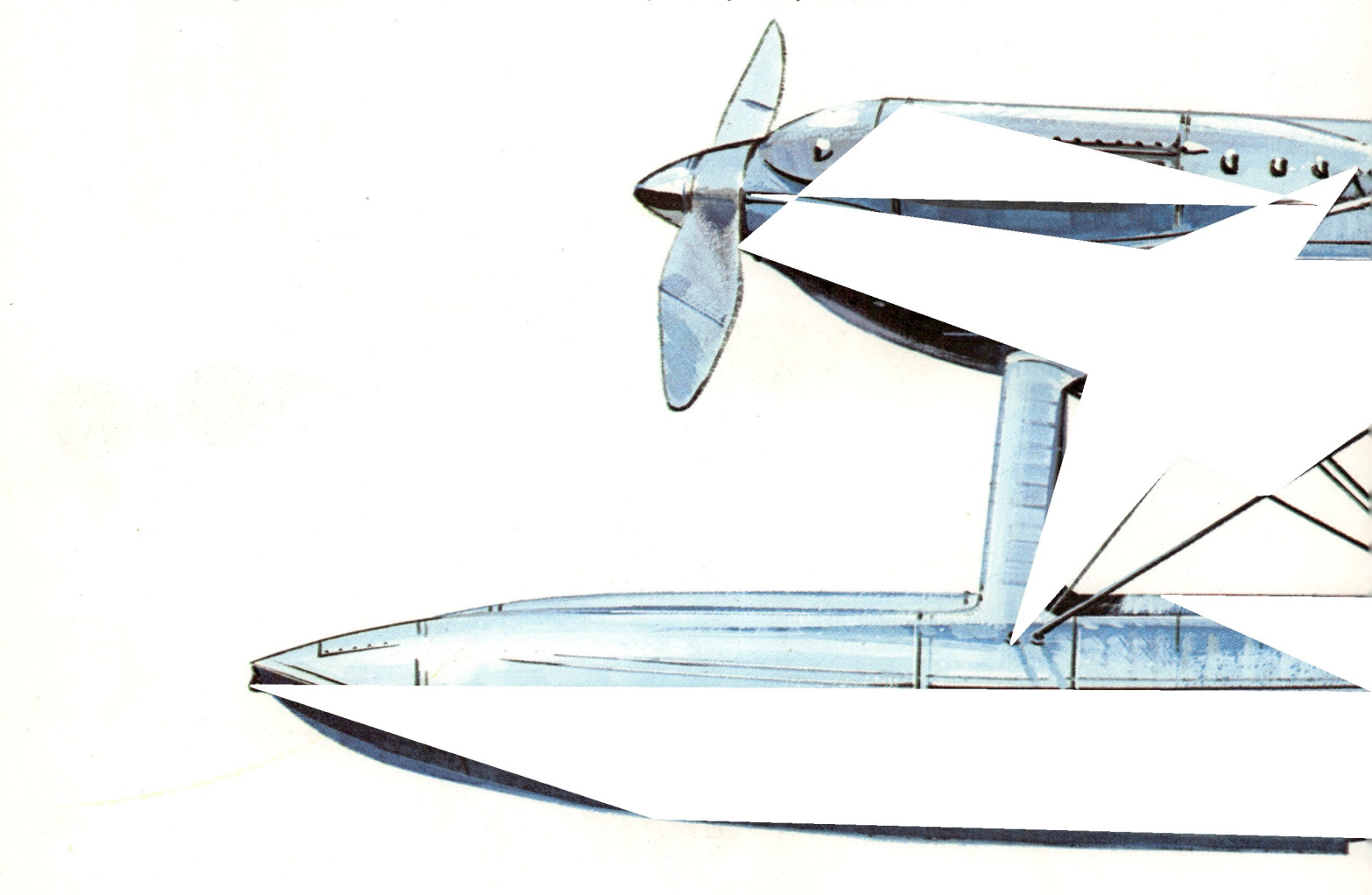

X-15
The X-15 has a rocket motor developing a thrust of 57,000 lbs. and has flown at over 4,000 m.p.h., reaching heights of over 50 miles. Pilots who fly as high as this qualify for astronaut's "wings."

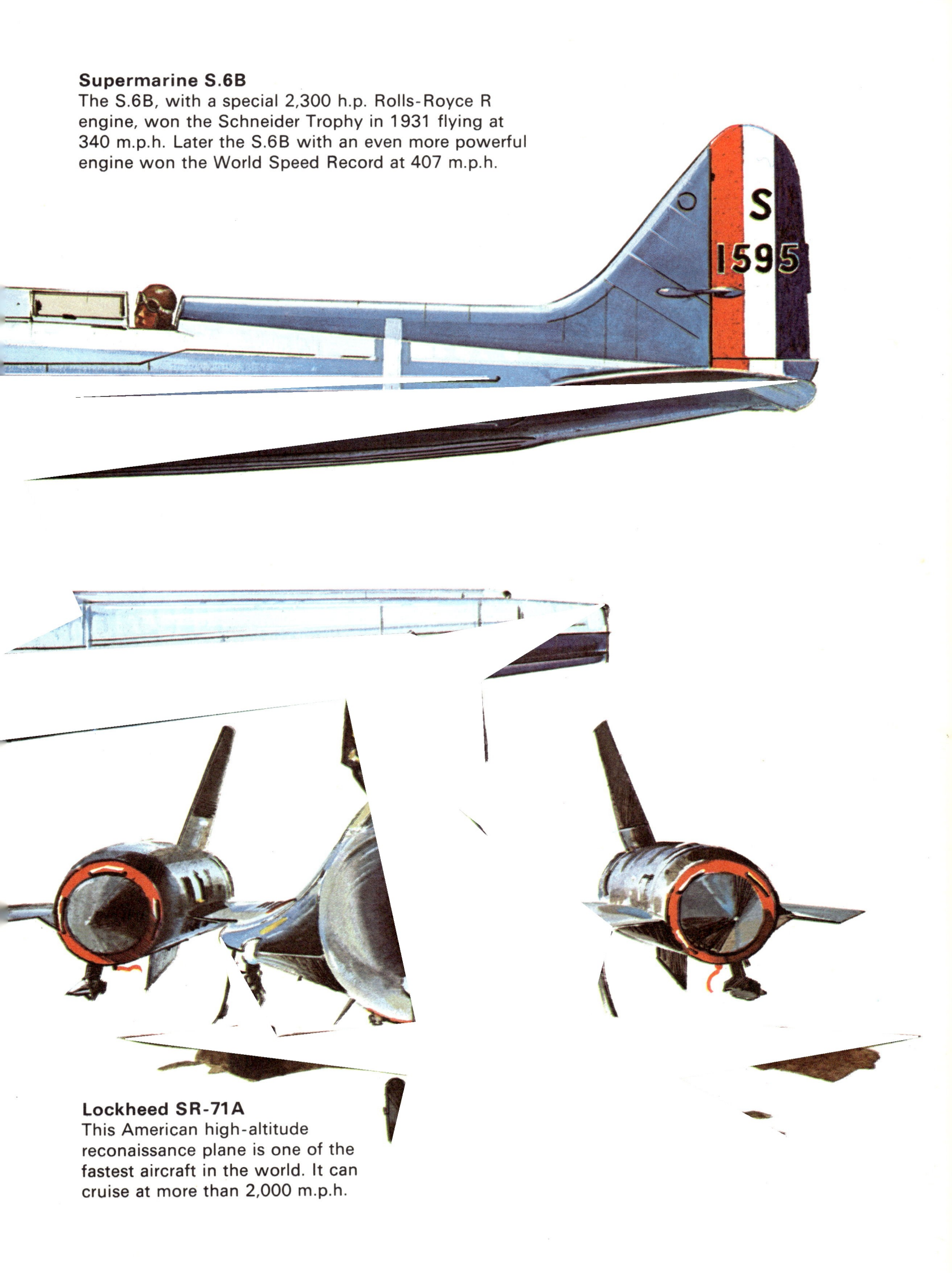

Supermarine S.6B
The S.6B, with a special 2,300 h.p. Rolls-Royce R engine, won the Schneider Trophy in 1931 flying at 340 m.p.h. Later the S.6B with an even more powerful engine won the World Speed Record at 407 m.p.h.

Lockheed SR-71A
This American high-altitude reconaissance plane is one of the fastest aircraft in the world. It can cruise at more than 2,000 m.p.h.

Planes for Testing

Special planes are often built to test a new idea. It is better to do this on a small and fairly cheap plane than on an expensive full-size aircraft, as the idea may prove impossible.

XB-70
Designed as a 2,000 m.p.h. bomber, the XB-70 was in fact used to test new systems while flying at three times the speed of sound.

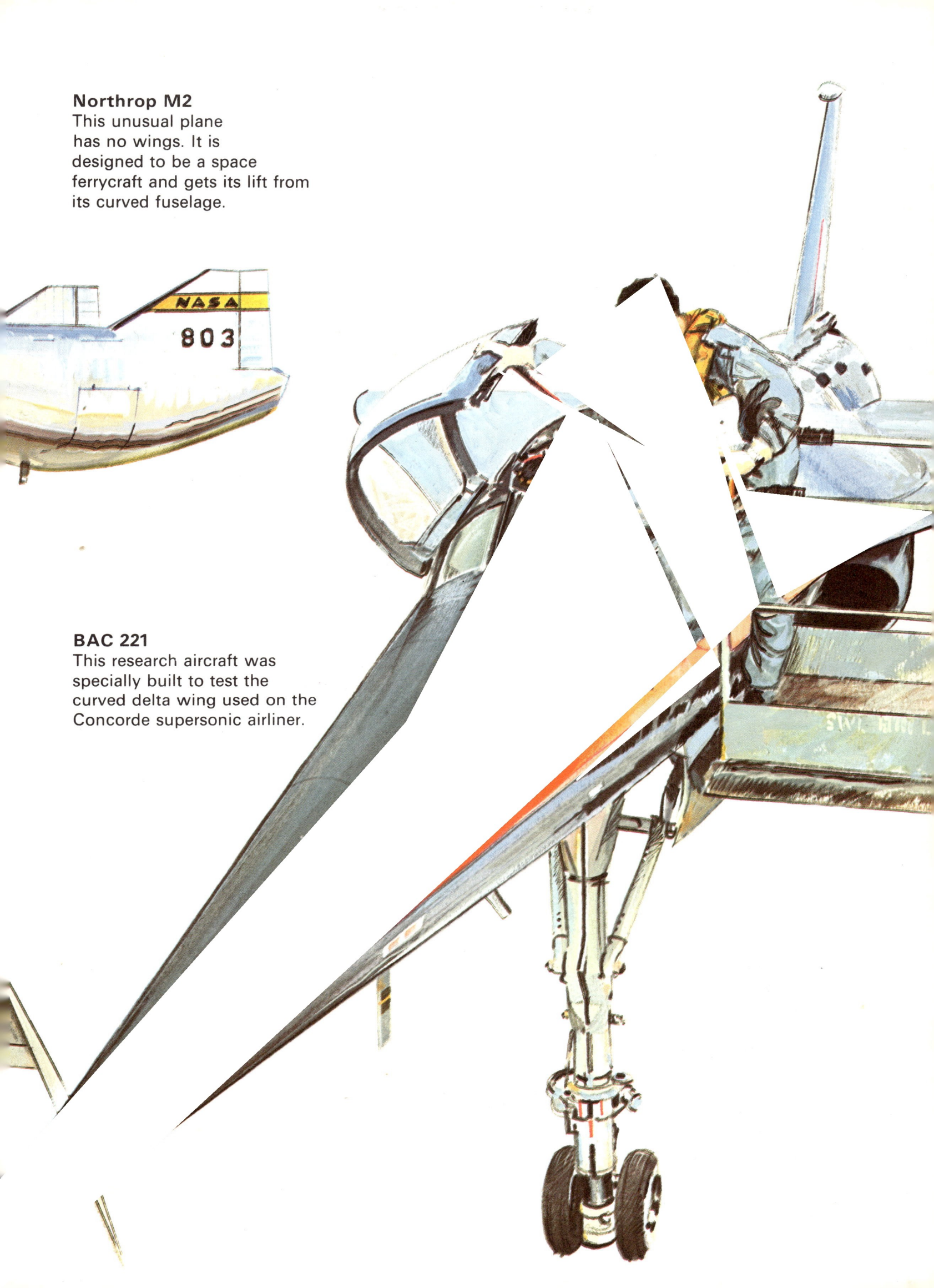

Northrop M2
This unusual plane has no wings. It is designed to be a space ferrycraft and gets its lift from its curved fuselage.

BAC 221
This research aircraft was specially built to test the curved delta wing used on the Concorde supersonic airliner.

Unusual Aircraft

Experimental aircraft that have been designed for special jobs often look very unusual, as can be seen from the four following examples.

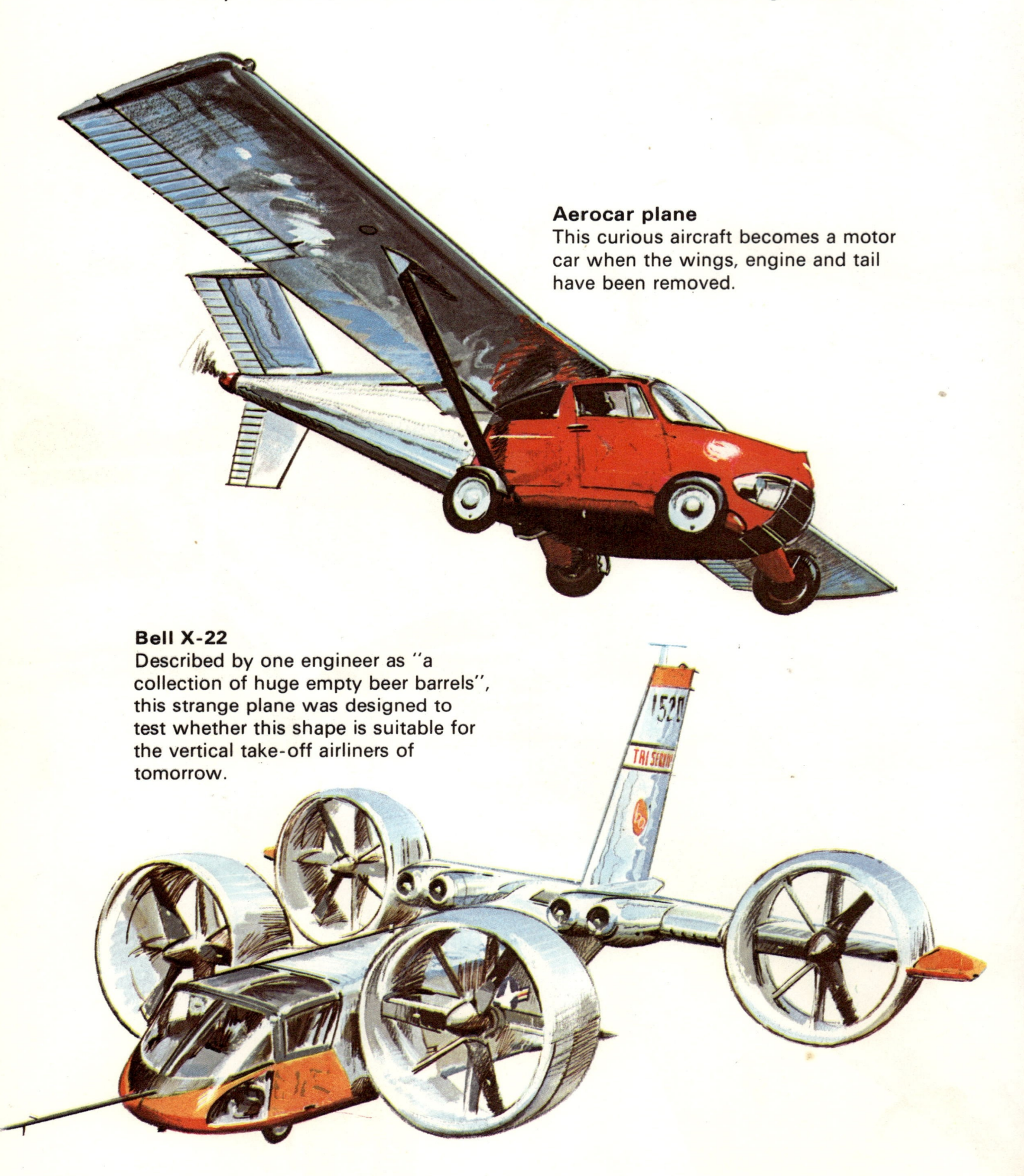

Aerocar plane
This curious aircraft becomes a motor car when the wings, engine and tail have been removed.

Bell X-22
Described by one engineer as "a collection of huge empty beer barrels", this strange plane was designed to test whether this shape is suitable for the vertical take-off airliners of tomorrow.

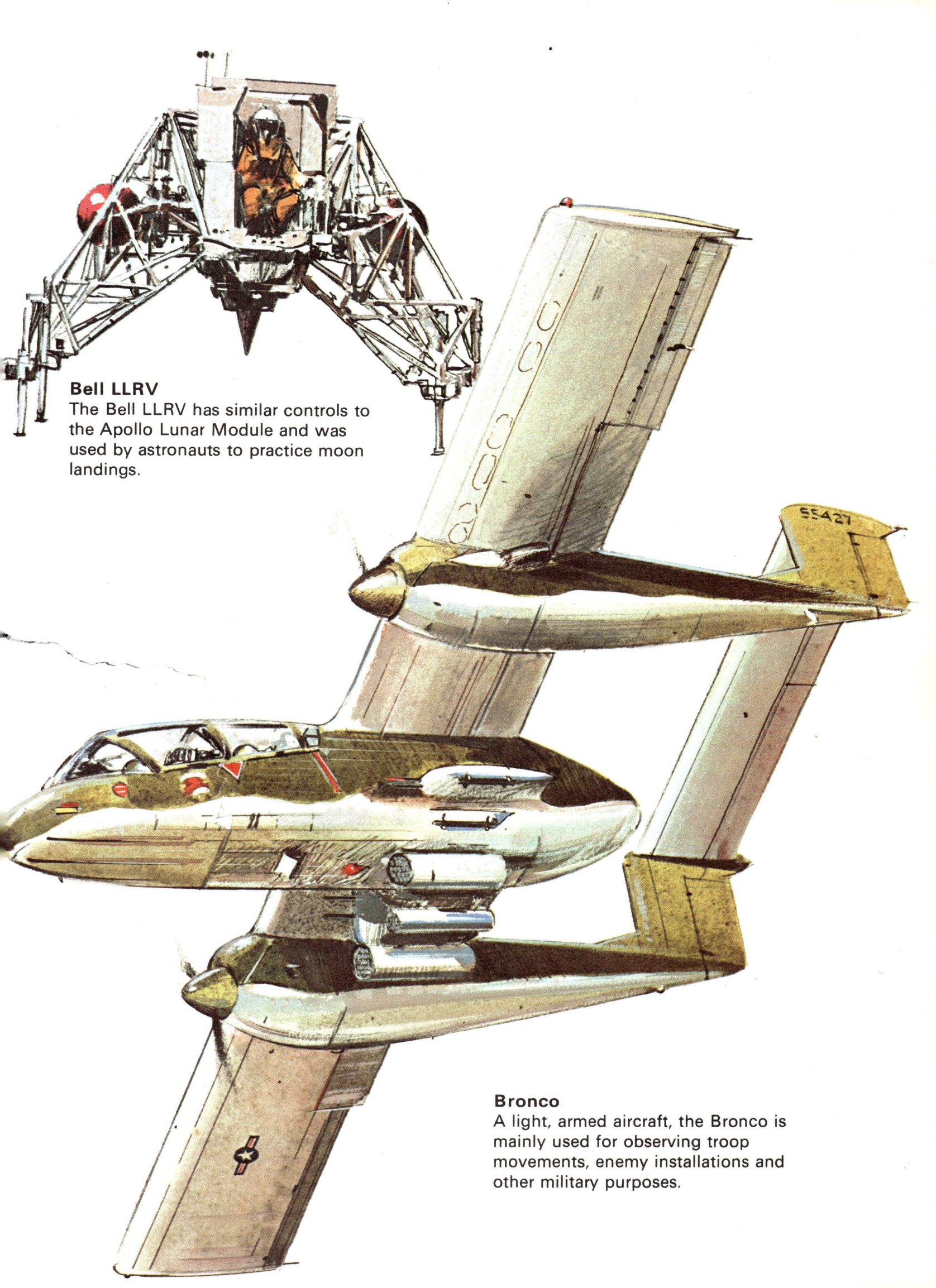

Bell LLRV
The Bell LLRV has similar controls to the Apollo Lunar Module and was used by astronauts to practice moon landings.

Bronco
A light, armed aircraft, the Bronco is mainly used for observing troop movements, enemy installations and other military purposes.

Flying for Fun

Most airplanes are built for work, or to serve with air forces. Only a few are built and used for the sheer fun of flying. These aircraft give their pilots thrills and pleasure unequalled by any other sport in the world.

Pup
The Pup is a popular club aircraft which is fully aerobatic. It can carry two adults and two children.

Thrush
The Thrush is an all-round Polish aircraft, popular with flying clubs and also used for a wide variety of jobs. The high wing gives passengers a really good view of the ground.

Tiger Moth
The Tiger Moth was in service with the Royal Air Force for 15 years. It is still a popular trainer and more people have flown themselves in Tiger Moths than any other plane.

Playmate
This handy plane has folding wings for easy storage and room enough for a pilot and two passengers.

Tilting Wings

Many experts believe that the aircraft of tomorrow will be able to take off and land vertically, like helicopters. In level flight, however, they will be able to fly as fast as a jet airliner. One way of enabling an aircraft to rise straight up and fly fast is to fit tilting wings.

Dynavert
Three of these Canadian aircraft have been built to test tilt-wing planes for reconnaissance, armed support and interurban airliners.

XC-142

This is the biggest tilting-wing aircraft in the world. It can carry up to thirty-two soldiers, with guns and equipment. For level flight the wing tilts down and the craft flies like a normal plane.

But for take-off and landing, the wing tilts up so that the propellers can pull the aircraft straight up. As illustrated here, the aircraft is shown in both horizontal and vertical flight.

Offices in the Clouds

Large companies own private aircraft so that factories and important customers can be visited at a moment's notice. Business planes are simply smaller versions of luxury passenger aircraft.

Jetstar
The American Lockheed Jetstar was one of the first business jets. It has four engines instead of the usual two and carries thirteen passengers.

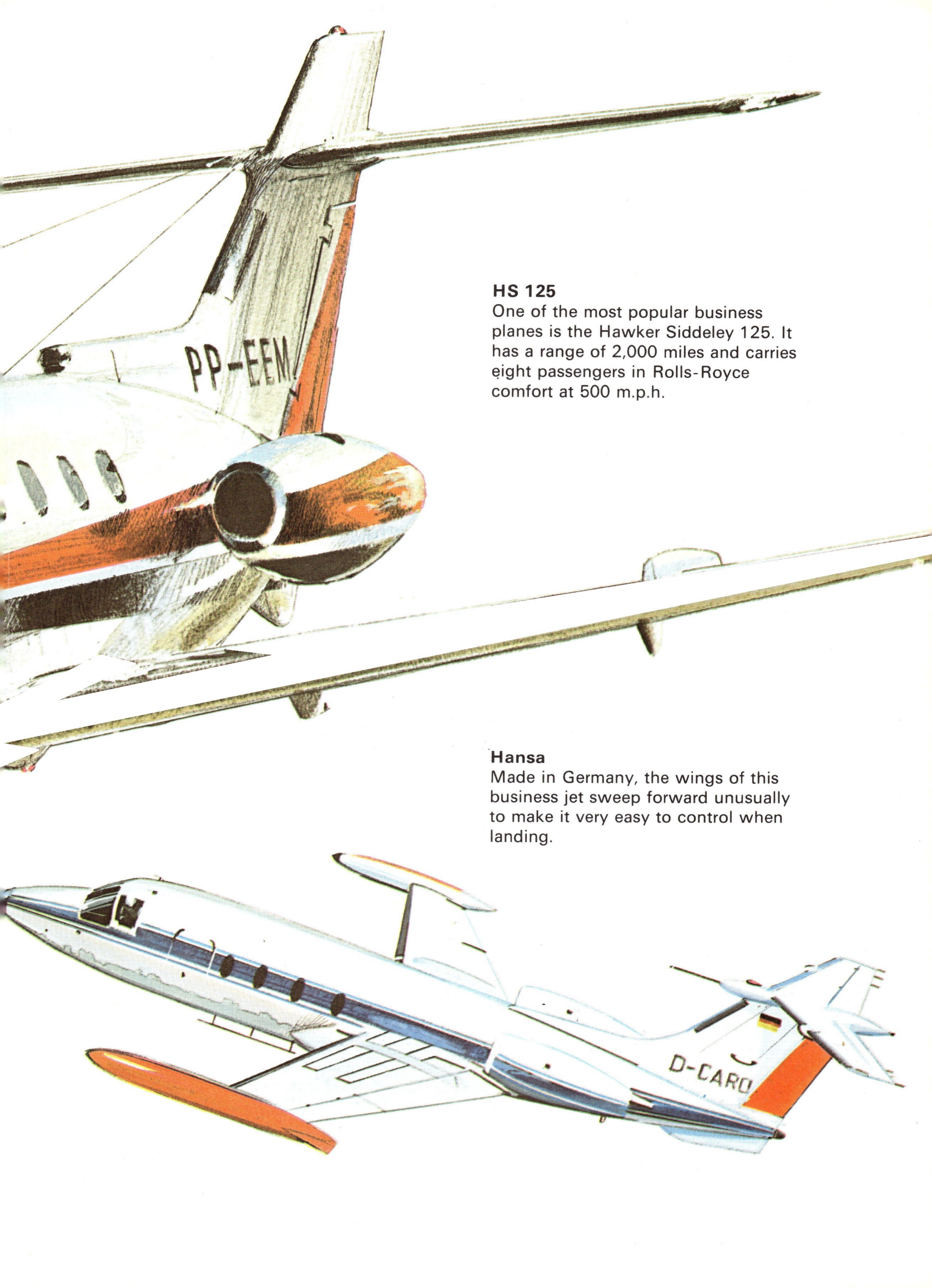

HS 125
One of the most popular business planes is the Hawker Siddeley 125. It has a range of 2,000 miles and carries eight passengers in Rolls-Royce comfort at 500 m.p.h.

Hansa
Made in Germany, the wings of this business jet sweep forward unusually to make it very easy to control when landing.

Swing-wing Aircraft

For high speeds, swept wings are necessary, but for landing and taking off, straight wings are better. Most airplanes have either swept or straight wings, but a small number can have both. They are aircraft with swing-wings.

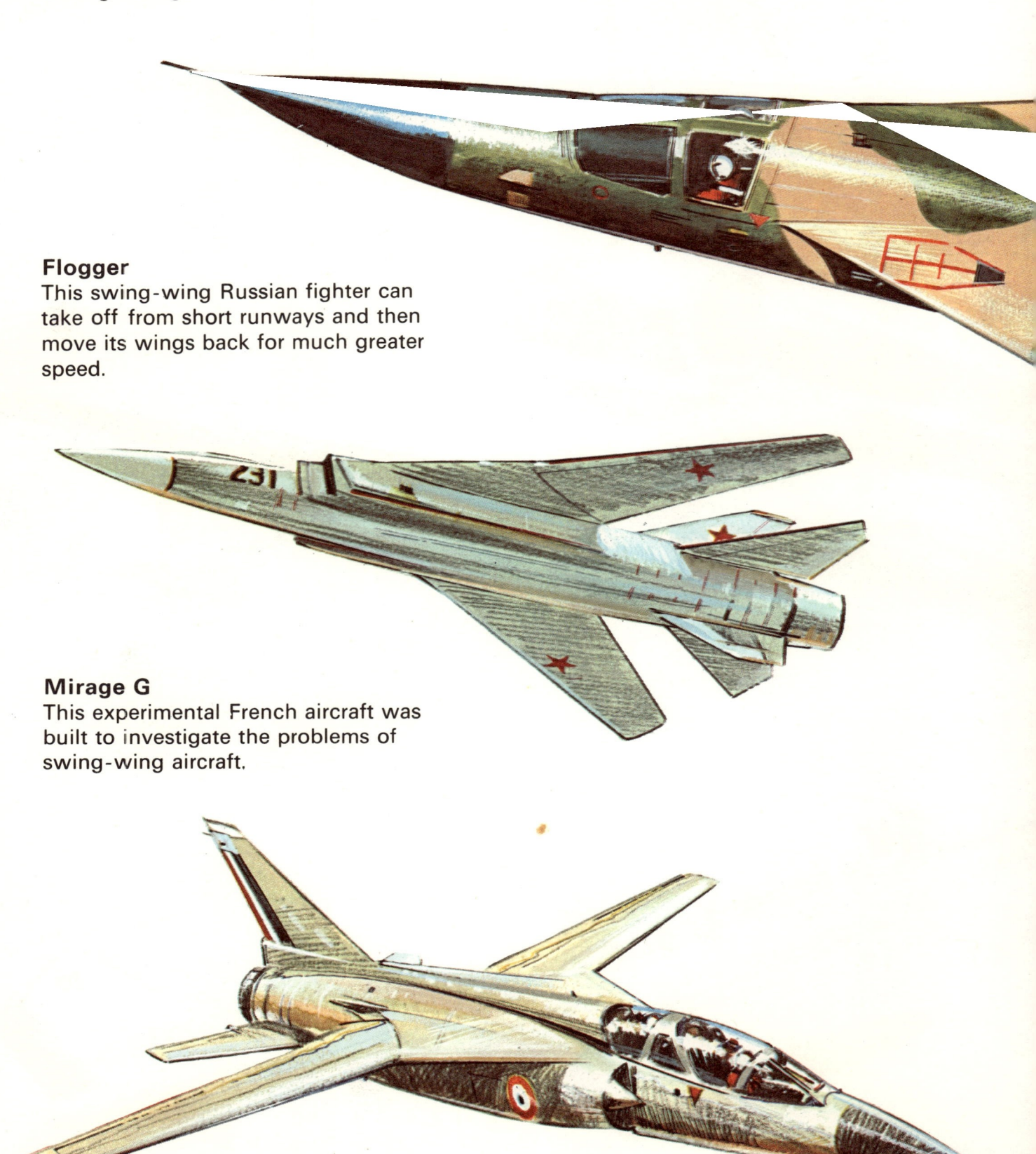

Flogger
This swing-wing Russian fighter can take off from short runways and then move its wings back for much greater speed.

Mirage G
This experimental French aircraft was built to investigate the problems of swing-wing aircraft.

General Dynamics F-111
This American swing-wing fighter can fly at nearly 1,800 m.p.h. The bomber version can carry up to fifty bombs, each weighing nearly half a ton. The illustration shows the two positions of the wings.

Jumbos of the Air

Since the Wright *Flyer* made its first historic flight in 1903, aircraft have become bigger and bigger and are carrying more and more people. Within the next few years, the age of the giant airliner will be with us. Carrying between 300 and 500 passengers, they well deserve their nick-name of jumbo-jet.

Antonov A-22
This huge military jumbo can carry between 200 and 300 fully equipped troops, or tanks, or other heavy weapons. A passenger, two-deck version, could carry 724 passengers.

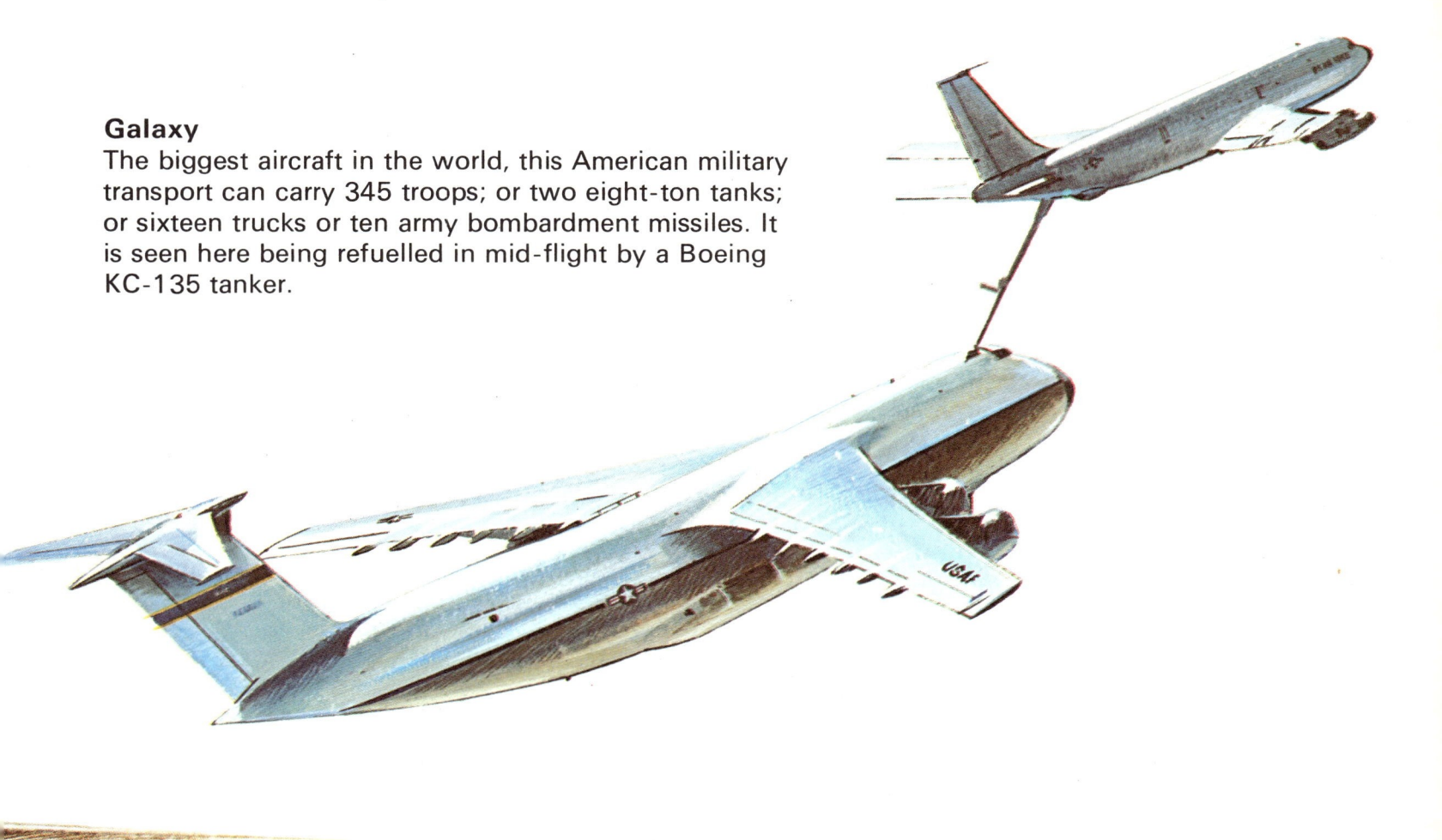

Galaxy
The biggest aircraft in the world, this American military transport can carry 345 troops; or two eight-ton tanks; or sixteen trucks or ten army bombardment missiles. It is seen here being refuelled in mid-flight by a Boeing KC-135 tanker.

Boeing 747
The first jumbo of the air, the Boeing 747 can carry up to 490 passengers. It is powered by four turbo-jet engines and its total length is 235 feet. The height of the tail assembly is 42½ feet. A staircase connects the main cabin with a compartment on the upper deck behind the cockpit.

Faster than Sound

At one time it was thought that aircraft could never fly faster than the speed of sound. Several planes broke up trying to pass through the sound barrier, (750 m.p.h.), but at last the problem was solved so that today, faster-than-sound flight is safe and smooth.

Mig 23
One of the best fighters in the world, the Russian Mig 23 can fly at nearly 2,000 m.p.h. and carry a heavy load of weapons.

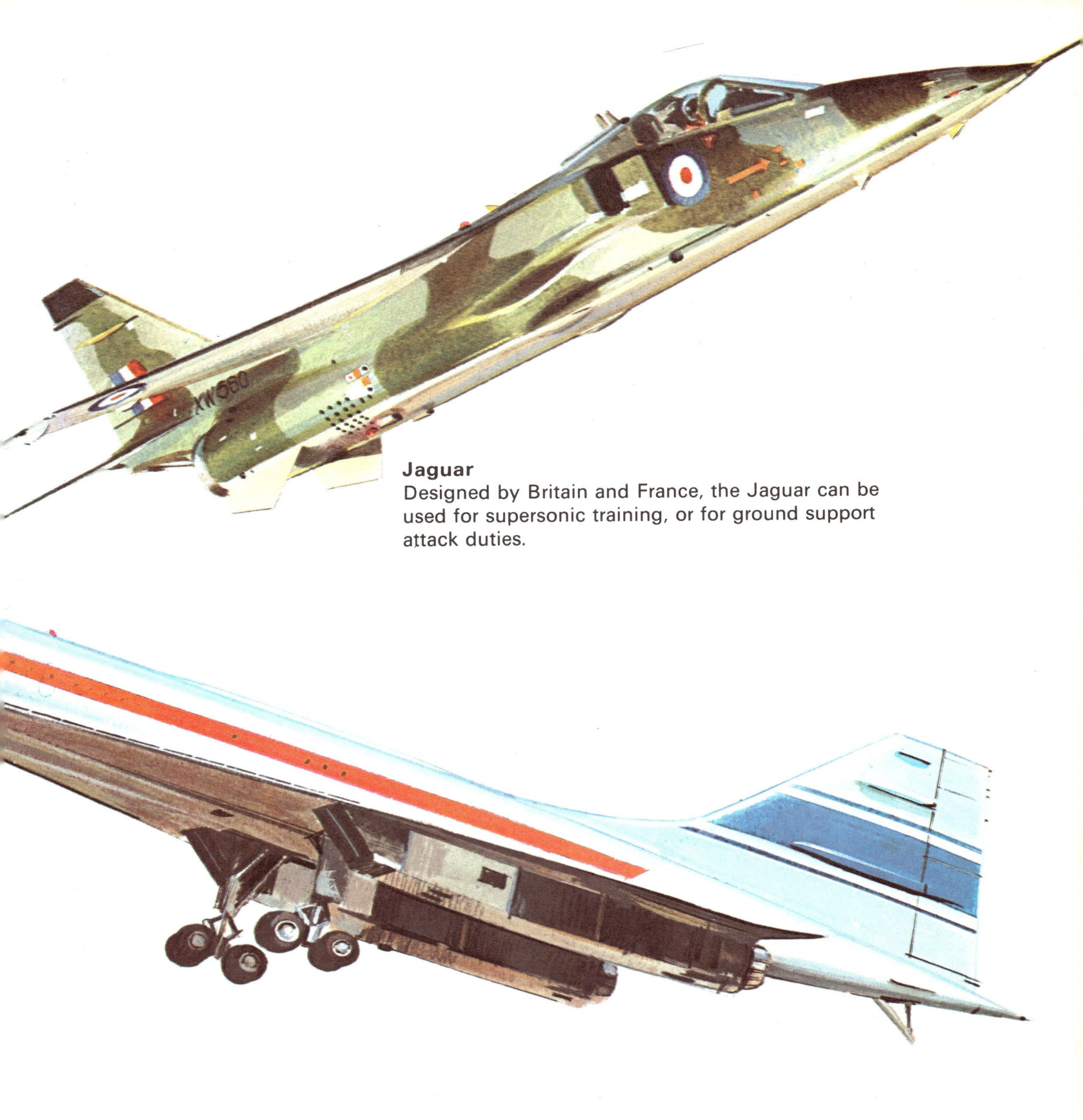

Jaguar
Designed by Britain and France, the Jaguar can be used for supersonic training, or for ground support attack duties.

Concorde
The supersonic airliner, designed by Britain and France, can carry up to 144 passengers across the Atlantic at 1,450 m.p.h. The pointed nose hinges down for take-off and landing, and when the aircraft is moving at less than the speed of sound.

Jump-Jets

At the present time, most airliners and military aircraft need long runways when landing and taking off. This means that airports are not only very expensive, but they cannot be built in the center of cities. Fighters and bomber aircraft need large airfields, too, but these can be attacked by an enemy. There are some aircraft which do not need long runways; these are the planes that can rise and land vertically. They are known as VTOL (Vertical Take-off and Landing) aircraft.

Harrier
In service with the Royal Air Force, this advanced VTOL fighter directs its engine thrust downwards for taking off, and backwards for normal level flight.

Mirage III-V
This experimental French jump-jet has eight lift engines in the fuselage and one engine in the tail for normal forward flight.

Do 31
The German Do 31 is the world's largest VTOL aircraft. The pods on the wing tips contain eight lift engines while the two under the wings are used for normal flight.

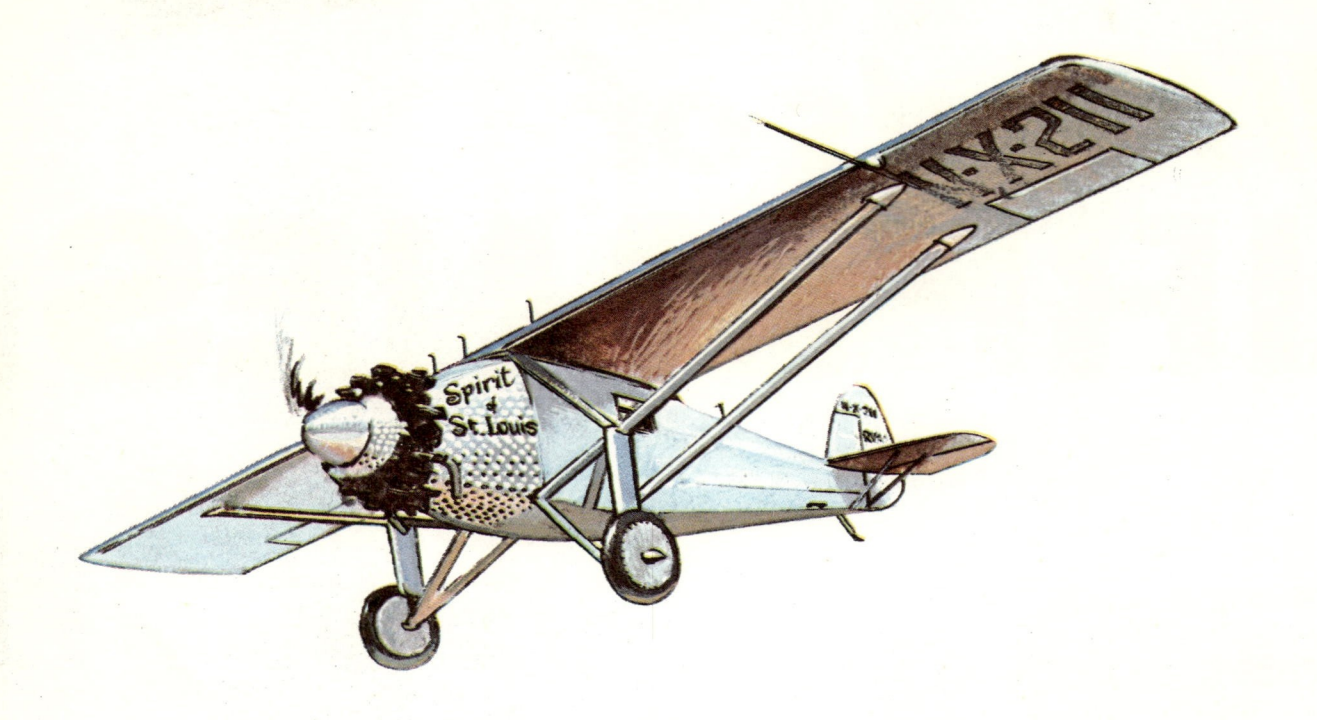

Library of Congress Catalog Card Number: 79-158765
ISBN: 0-448-02659-7 (Trade Edition)
ISBN: 0-448-04293-2 (Library Edition)

Original edition published under the title, *All Sorts of Aircraft,* by the Hamlyn Publishing Group, Limited.

Copyright © Golden Treasure Books, Limited, 1970.

Published in 1971 in the United States by Grosset & Dunlap, Inc., New York. All rights reserved.

Printed and bound in the United States.